Dear

Elvis

Toni McCloe

Dear Elvis

Dear Elvis
Copyright © 2017 by Toni McCloe. All rights reserved.

No part of this book may be reproduced, stored in a retrieval system or transmitted in any way by any means, electronic, mechanical, photocopy, recording or otherwise without the prior permission of the author except as provided by USA copyright law.

Published in the United States of America
ISBN: 978-1-52196-914-4
Grief, Death & Dying, Love & Relationships
17.07.31

Dedication

For my grandchildren: Michael, Jacquelyn, Robert, Brian, Stephen, Tori, Carey, Rory, Owen and Chloe

And for Don

TABLE OF CONTENTS

Epigraph

Part 1:

If I Can Dream

Part 2:

What Now My Love

Part 3:

The Impossible Dream

Epigraph

Sometimes signs come from other dimensions to make your life a little better, a little kinder, a little more musical.

Annie Kagan

Part 1

If I Can Dream

Give sorrow words; the grief that does not speak whispers the o'erfraught heart and bids it break.

William Shakespeare

1.

Dear Elvis,

I'm sorry that you're dead. Forty-two was much too young to die and you have been dead for such a long time. But then dead is dead, or at least that's what a writing instructor told me once. He said there are no comparative or superlative forms for dead. There is no dead, deader, deadest. There is only just dead. But then I'll bet you already knew that.

So listen Elvis, where are you? Are you in heaven? And if you are, where is heaven? To tell you the truth, I kind of believe in heaven. So there must be one. I just don't know where it is and I kind of figured you would know since, well, you know, you've been there for forever. And you must know everybody. Like, do you meet everyone after they arrive? Everyone who knew you? Or knew of you?

Let me get to the point. Is Don there? Have you seen him? Have you talked to him? I'll bet you have. He really liked you, you know. Maybe not as much as he liked Engelbert or Goulet. Oh right, I forgot. Don didn't really like Robert Goulet, and come to think of it, neither did you. You didn't think much of his singing, and you once threw a shoe at a TV when Goulet was on. You did that a lot, didn't you? Threw shoes at the TV and then you had to buy another and another and another TV? Oh, wait! It wasn't a shoe. What was I thinking? It was a bullet. You used to shoot the TV whenever Goulet was on.

That wasn't very cool, you know. I know they didn't have remotes back then, but you could have gotten up to change the channel or gotten one of the guys to do it for you. Shooting TVs wouldn't fly very well in today's world. People frown on guns today. They aren't considered macho cool the way they used to be.

So listen, do me a favor and think about what I asked you. See if you can come up with something. I kind of really need to know if there is a heaven, and where it is, and I'm sort of counting on you to tell me.

Oh, and if you see Don, tell him – well, just tell him I said hello.

Sincerely,

Toni

2.

Dear Elvis,

I miss my buddy. I miss my friend. I miss the man who once called me the love of his life and who was the love of mine. Once, we were so close that when asked about the relationship between us, I jokingly told someone he and I were Siamese twins separated at birth. Never once did I think what it would be like to be separated by death.

When he died I felt so deeply and intensely lost that for weeks no other thoughts entered my mind. Two days after he died I dreamt I was standing inside his house and, even though I was aware that he was gone, I felt great peace even in the moments just after awakening.

Afterward however, I began again to struggle with his death as though it were some kind of ancient dragon I had to fight and defeat before I could even begin to feel better. And even as I struggled with his death, I tried to deny it, unable to form a simple sentence that would contain both his name and the word 'died' in it.

Then, when the memories began to return, I started thinking of all of the places we had been to together, and I began driving around compulsively until I realized I was looking, not for more memories, but for him somehow believing that if I could just look for him long enough I would find him.

One day while I was driving I heard a song on the radio about a guy who wanted to be taken to a place where it's "Sunny and 75," and I remembered all the hours I had spent with this man in a room where the blinds were always halfway up. And I remembered how, whenever I was with him, it was always sunny and seventy-five for me.

I miss him, Elvis. Sometimes I miss him so much I feel as though I have lost my twin. Oh, I'm sorry. I forgot. I forgot about you and your twin. I forgot about how much you missed him. People probably didn't believe that. They probably didn't believe you could miss someone you'd never even met, but I believed it. I still believe it.

I felt like that when I met Don. I felt as though I'd always known him. Even before we met. But not in the womb, sometime before that. Is there a time before that?

Sincerely,

Toni

3.

Dear Elvis,

I read somewhere that in heaven people look the way they did on earth in their twenties. Personally, I think you looked your best in your thirties during your Las Vegas years. But maybe that's what people mean when they say "beauty is in the eye of the beholder." What is it about people that gets them – us – so hung up on looks?

Anyway, I have the feeling I will recognize you no matter what you look like in heaven. God knows I've stared at your pictures long enough. But what about Don? Even though I didn't meet him until late in life, he was beautiful, Elvis, with his full head of hair and the curl that fell to the middle of his forehead. But I wonder if I will recognize him if he looks the way he did when he was twenty-something?

Of course, like me, he had been married before. There was a picture of him and his wife sitting on a table in the hallway between his bedroom and the TV room. That picture must have been taken when they were both in their twenties. Maybe right after they were married. They both looked so radiant.

"You look like an actor," I told him the first time I saw it. At that moment however, I couldn't think of the name of the actor he resembled. "Who do you look like?" I asked while he looked at me as though I were kidding, this man who once asked, "Why me? Why did you pick me? I'm ordinary."

It was my turn then to look at him as though *he* were kidding. "Not to me," I told him. "Cornel Wilde!" I said triumphantly now that I remembered the actor's name. "You look just like Cornel Wilde did in *The Greatest Show on Earth*."

"I've heard that before." he said dryly, matter of factly, and I laughed.

Dear Elvis, I've been thinking that it may help you to find him if I told you a little bit more about him so you'll know who you're looking for, except I can't do that yet. I can't separate him from me. When I think of him, when I thought of him, it was always as the other half of me and it's so hard to separate the two of us and to look at just him. But I'll try, Elvis. I promise I'll try. Maybe the next time I write.

Sincerely,

Toni

4.

Dear Elvis,

I guess you must be wondering why I picked you to write to. I mean, of all the people who've ever lived, why you? And I guess a part of it is because I feel closer to you than I do to anyone else who's dead. I feel closer to you because, well, because I fell in love with you once. Although, actually it was twice.

The first time was when I was fourteen and you were twenty-one and just getting started. I found you on the *Ed Sullivan Show* one Sunday night late in 1956. The "Toast of the Town" they used to call Ed Sullivan back then, the town being New York City. My dad really loved that show. He used to watch it every Sunday night until it became some kind of a ritual for him. Sometimes I watched it too, because in those days there was only one television set per household and if you wanted to watch it, you watched whatever your parents were watching.

It wasn't too bad really, unless there were a bunch of jugglers on it or something like that, and then it all seemed very geeky. Although we didn't say geeky back then. We used to say "square." We used to say square and use our fingers to draw a square in the air. We thought we were so cool. I'm sure you remember that. You probably did it too.

Actually, isn't that what the very flamboyant Liberace did once when the two of you were on stage together? Didn't he draw a square in the air and then point to you, making everybody (including you) laugh out loud? "Mr. Showmanship" they called him. Elvis, did you know that, like you, Liberace had a twin who died at birth?

Anyway, to be honest, I didn't just happen to be watching that night. Some of the kids at school had seen you during one of your earlier TV appearances, and they were all talking about you so much I decided to look for you that night.

Up until then I had been listening to songs on the radio like Patti Page's "How Much is that Doggie in the Window," but when I sat down in front of the television and saw you perform that night, it didn't seem so much as though you were appearing on stage, but as though you were exploding onto it.

You sang three songs and then, after a ventriloquist's act, you came back and sang two more. Up until then, the camera was showing you only from the waist up, but when you started your last song, it zoomed out revealing all of you.

With your hips swiveling and your legs moving, you grabbed hold of the microphone and pulled it in close. Then you smiled that smile of yours, which somehow made you look both shy and sly simultaneously, and as though you had the world on a string. But most of all, you looked as though you were having the time of your life. (Which, come to think of it, was exactly how I felt after meeting Don.)

Later, a lot of things would be written and said about your earliest TV appearances. A lot of people were going to try to explain what it was that made you a superstar. But of all the things written and said about you, it was Bruce Springsteen, I think, who said it best when he said, "it was like he came along and whispered some dream in everybody's ear and somehow we all dreamed it."

But there's another quote I love about you. This one is by Marion Keisker, the woman who worked at Sun Studios with Sam Phillips. Marion was lucky because she got to know you before you were famous. Her image of you, she said, "was as a child." She said you were "like a mirror" in that whenever you performed, whatever anyone was looking for, they would find in you.

Anyway, after watching you that night, I went from listening to songs like Perry Como's "Hot Diggity (Dog Diggity Boom)" to

20

listening to "Hound Dog" - and so did a whole lot of other people. The change was drastic. Too drastic for some, like pastors and parents, and even some disc jockeys. Some of whom wanted to hang you in effigy. Some of whom wanted to hang you in person. Many of them would have too, Elvis, had it not been for what Ed Sullivan said – telling the world you were a "real fine decent" human being, which is what I discovered for myself the second time I fell in love with you.

Sincerely,

Toni

5.

Dear Elvis,

Have you found him yet? Have you seen him? In case you haven't, I can tell you a little bit more about him now. I think I can go back to the beginning and tell you how we met and a little bit more about the relationship we shared.

Most of all, Don was a good man. He was a sweet man who laughed a lot with others – with the people who were closest to him and even, at times, with strangers. He never changed the world, but then he never wanted to. He pretty much liked it the way it was – which, to my great relief, was how he thought about me, too.

When we met, it was not long after the start of the new millennium. Do you remember that, Elvis? I mean I know you weren't here and that you weren't alive, and that time doesn't matter much where you are, but do you remember Y2K? Did you understand its significance?

There were so many people, down here on earth, who normally were not very superstitious, but who were afraid that night. They were afraid it was the end of the world, or that all the computers and clocks would fail, making it the end of time, and I have to admit that I was afraid, too.

Like a lot of people, I had gone out ahead of time and stocked up on a whole lot of canned goods and batteries and bottled water. I was just as afraid as anyone else, even if I couldn't identify what it was I was afraid of, or why I was stocking up on supplies. But by the time we got to early evening – even before midnight, I was fine.

I was fine because I had been watching Peter Jennings on television all afternoon. Jennings, as you may remember, was a news anchor back then and I watched with him as the new millennium was ushered in somewhere in the South Pacific by a group of natives who were so peaceful and quiet and serene, unlike the rest of us, unlike those of us who were supposed to be so civilized, unlike those of us who had been running around for days and weeks as though we were chickens who had already lost our heads.

So I wasn't afraid anymore. By the time the clock struck midnight, I was nice and relaxed and not feeling desperate, and not desperate to have my last good time before it all ended, before everything ended.

It wasn't long after that when I went to work for the local school district, and that's where I met Don. When we met, he was seven years older than I was, and he once said he thought he was too old for me, which only made me laugh. It wasn't as though we were kids, when a ten-year difference in age would have been practically insurmountable. Oh, I'm sorry, Elvis. I forgot about you and Priscilla. I forgot that Priscilla was only fourteen when you met and you were twenty-four, but then again, perhaps there are marriages in which ten years doesn't make much of a difference.

Actually, when I was a kid my best friend's father was ten years older than her mother and theirs was a strong marriage. Of course, it helped a lot that my friend's mother had a sense of humor and that she could laugh a lot – at herself as well as at others. Sometimes she would be sitting with us, my friend and me, and she would burst – for no apparent reason that either I or my friend could see – into peals of laughter.

Was that it, Elvis? Did Priscilla lack a sense of humor? No. It must have been deeper than that. You were always away in Hollywood and Priscilla must have been lonely. There is nothing deadlier to a marriage than when one person is lonely and the other is not. I was lonely all of my life until I met Don.

Sincerely,

Toni

6.

Dear Elvis,

Although I was living with my daughter Cindi when Don died, when we met I was living in the mother-in-law suite in the basement of my youngest daughter's house. While I lived downstairs, Jessi lived upstairs with her husband and four kids. I had been living there ever since I called her one day to tell her how much I hated the job I had, working at a bank. "Quit," she said, "and you can come live with us. Instead of working, you can do all of the cooking."

Back then, Jessi was driving a school bus and for a while that arrangement was working. Or at least I thought it was working until the day she came home and told me the school district was looking for another driver. I told her she was crazy. I told her there was no way I was going to start driving a school bus.

"What? Why? It's easy," she said.

"But those buses. They're so – long."

"You really don't have to worry about that," she assured me. "You just have to drive the front of the bus. The back always follows the front." I laughed at that and told her again she was crazy. But after thinking about it for a while, I decided to try it. I started driving in April and, right away, I loved it. I loved the hours – the early mornings and late afternoons, and having the rest of the day to myself.

When I started, a gray-haired woman named Mary, who had the mouth of a sailor and a heart of gold, taught me my run. Naturally we talked a lot, or at least she did. When she asked how long it had been since my divorce and I told her, she said twenty-five years was much too long to be alone. Then she added, "I know who you'd like," and even though she mentioned Don by name, I had no idea who it was she was talking about, although I have to admit I was curious. Before I could figure out who he was, however, summer arrived and the school year ended.

That was the summer when a doctor told me I had a lump in my breast and I was scared. Scared enough to sit down and to really think about my life and to start trying to make some kind of sense out of it.

It was hot that summer. There were days when the temperatures rose to above one hundred degrees. Despite this, I spent a good deal of my time outdoors, sitting under an old maple tree in our backyard and writing in my journal. I spent a lot of time writing about my childhood.

As difficult as writing about my childhood was, it was a whole lot easier than writing about my failed marriage. I tried writing about it several times, but with each attempt the memories eluded me, especially when I got to the part where the infidelities began. So I gave up trying to make sense of it all.

After getting the results of the biopsy and learning the mass was benign, I decided to accept Cindi's invitation to travel with her and her family to the Outer Banks of North Carolina.

On the first morning after our arrival, I got up early and walked to the beach to watch the sun as it rose in the sky looking like some gigantic and glorious peach. I watched until it slipped behind a cloud and then reappeared, this time looking like a shimmering ball of golden light shining upon the icy blue waters below where the waves crested and fell, each one finally erupting into tiny bubbles of joy.

I spent most of that week sitting on the beach writing about the sun and the sky and the sea. I sat there for hours, taking in the breadth and the depth of the ocean, acutely aware that for me all of it would end soon. But before it did, I wanted to breathe it all in, deeply.

On another day as I stood on the beach watching the horizon, I noticed that a few feet to my right and a few feet to my left, the sea and the sky seemed to blend together. Directly in front of me I saw a thin, vibrant strip of light at the exact spot where the sea and the sky met. I picked up the binoculars my son-in-law brought along to watch the dolphins, and as I looked more closely at that strip of light, which was as bright as quicksilver, I tried to determine if it was real or if it was just a figment of my imagination. And, as I searched the points where it began and ended, it slowly disappeared.

Later that night, in the middle of the night, I was awakened by a storm whose sudden bursts of thunder and bolts of lightning split the sky in two as it continued for more than an hour. As I watched all of this, I continued writing about it, hoping to paint a picture with my words. But it wasn't until after I returned home and read what I'd written that I realized the sun and the sea and the sky had become metaphors for the things I no longer remembered, and for the things that existed no longer, except perhaps along the outer banks of my mind.

Elvis, what do you remember? Do you remember what it's like to look out at the ocean and to feel as though you're looking at infinity? Do you remember what it's like to sit by the ocean and play? Or dream? Or sleep? Do you remember – of course you remember what it's like to be alone and to feel so lonesome you could cry.

Sincerely,

Toni

7.

Dear Elvis,

After leaving North Carolina I returned home feeling refreshed and ready to start the new school year. In September and October I had down time early every morning during which I would go back to the bus garage to report to our dispatcher, Nick.

At first I stayed in my bus and reported by radio. Then one day I noticed another driver had parked his bus outside the front door. I went inside and saw the other driver sitting at a desk, talking to Nick. And that's the first time I saw him, the first time I noticed him.

After that, I started going inside every morning, mostly to stand in the doorway and to listen as the two men talked. Then one morning I found myself alone with Don and decided to ask him a question. When I asked my question he was standing about three feet away from me. As he answered he started walking toward me, coming so close that by the time he finished he was standing inside my personal space. At which point, he stopped and smiled.

On another morning, just before Thanksgiving, my bus broke down and Nick sent Don to rescue me. On the way back to the bus garage we had a few minutes alone during which he told me he was a widower and that his wife had died of breast cancer five years earlier.

Later, after the relationship between us began, I bought a card which on the outside said, "I know exactly what it was you said that made me fall in love with you," and on the inside it said, "I think it was 'hi.'" I laughed when I read that, thinking it was more than likely a two-syllable word like "hello."

One morning just after Thanksgiving, I got to work early and was standing in front of the drivers' bulletin board. I was looking at the list of schools closed for each day, wondering if any of them were mine when Don came through the front door and stood beside me. I must have been standing there too long because suddenly he looked at me, then back at the list. He raised his hand and put his finger on the date. "There aren't any?" he said.

To which I responded with something like, "Huh?"

He laughed, and with his finger still on the date, he said, "There aren't any school closings. See. Today's the fourth."

"Oh. I hadn't even gotten that far," I said, and he laughed again.

At first I was hesitant about falling in love, but as time progressed I began to trust the situation more. *Enough!* I kept telling myself. *Don't go there.* And yet, I was curiously willing "to go there," even eager to go there. By mid-December I was seeing him everywhere, at the time clock, in the garage, and even on the road. Whenever we ran into one another we would smile, shyly at first, and then more broadly, each of us looking as though we were keeping a secret the other didn't know. After that, my behavior began to change dramatically as I found myself tripping over my own two feet and grinning from ear to ear until my fourteen-year old grandson demanded to know if all teenage girls behaved the way I did.

Don's best friend was a man named Luke, who used to join him on his bus every morning so the two of them could sit and talk before starting their runs. One day, Luke invited me along and during the next few months Don and I became friends. And then one morning when I was sitting in the lounge, Don walked in, saw me, and held my gaze even as he walked across the room, making me feel as though a question had been asked and answered.

Sometimes at night I would take out my journal and write about what was happening between us. "Dear Dov," I wrote one evening (Dov being the name I had given my journal when I was a teenager, naming it after a character in Leon Uris' *Exodus*), "Sometimes I feel as though there is some magnetic force between us, and while I feel that he feels it too, he seems reluctant to take the relationship further."

So I decided to do it myself, inviting both Don and Luke to dinner at my apartment. When they accepted I was ecstatic. That dinner on February 2, 2002 - exactly twelve years before his death - went off without a hitch, especially after Don lifted his wineglass and, looking only at me, spoke a toast that left me breathless.

The next day he call to thank me and to invite me to have dinner again with him – and with Luke. My hand was on the telephone when it rang. We were still using land lines then, and I was about to make a call myself when it rang. It startled me so much I picked it up just to make it stop ringing. When I said hello I must have said it a little too gruffly.

"Did it even ring?" he asked, making me laugh. Then, "It's Don." As we talked, I must have said something funny because I remember hearing him laugh out loud.

Once, after we'd been together for a while, I turned to him and said as lovers sometimes do, "I wish we had met sooner."

"We did meet sooner," he replied.

"No, we didn't."

"But we did," he insisted. "Don't you remember? Jessi got sick one day. It was a couple of months before you started working. When she got sick I drove her home and you drove me back to my car."

"That was you?"

He looked at me quizzically then, and was a little miffed, I think, that I hadn't remembered him. Then he said he'd tried to hit on me that day, but that I'd been too dense to notice. (I can just hear him now, "I never said 'hit on.'" Well, maybe not, Elvis. But it was close. It was definitely close.)

The last time we talked was just a few days before he died. What I remember most about that call was that he laughed out loud just like he did the first time he called.

I have to stop writing now, Elvis. My cell phone is ringing. It rang a minute ago and it jarred me so much I just sat there staring at it, wishing it could somehow be Don.

Sincerely,

Toni

8.

Dear Elvis,

On Valentine's Day he gave me some candy and I gave him a card in which I had placed a poem I'd written a day or two earlier. When he asked, "Should I open this now or save it for later?" I could barely answer. Then with a smile he said, "I'll save it for later."

But when later came he told me he wasn't ready for romance. He said he wasn't healthy enough for romance. He said he'd had prostate cancer – and congestive heart failure. He said he had hypertension. And diabetes.

I didn't know what prostate cancer was. I didn't understand congestive heart failure. I wasn't worried about diabetes. Or hypertension.

I thought he was perfect.

We were together for the first time in March and in April he told me he loved me. He said that again, and again, and again, and then he stopped telling me that, although by then it didn't matter much because I knew that he loved me. I saw it in his eyes whenever he looked at me and I heard it in his voice every time he spoke to me.

Sincerely,

Toni

9.

Dear Elvis,

Before we go any further, there is something I have to tell you. But when I do I don't want you to get mad at me. I don't want you to do anything. Except listen.

There are a lot of people who remember exactly where they were and what they were doing on the day that you died, but I wasn't one of them. Actually Elvis, I lost track of you long before that day. Do you remember how, when you were drafted, you were afraid all of your fans would forget you while you were away? Well, I have to confess that I was one of those fans.

I know. I know, Elvis. The last thing I remember of you was seeing your first movie, *Love Me Tender,* at a local theater. And yes, I *was* one of those crazy teenage girls who, upon seeing you die at the end of the movie, went rushing toward the screen crying hysterically. I'm sorry to say I didn't even see your second movie, *Loving You.*

By the time you got out of the service, I was about to enter a convent. Wait! Didn't one of your co-stars shock all of Hollywood – the whole world actually – when she went into a convent? Dolores Hart. That was her name. I wonder what ever happened to her. I'm going to look her up on my computer. Everything's on the computer, Elvis. Everything.

After that, I lost track of you again. Oh, I listened to your music, but I completely missed your Las Vegas years. By then the marriage I had entered was headed for divorce. Let's just say that losing track of you was not the only thing I missed during those years. When you died I'm not sure if the kids and I even had a television, and it wasn't until a long time afterward that my brain registered your death. After my divorce, I went back to Temple University in Philadelphia to get my degree. Then I started working at a small weekly newspaper, taking a bus to the office.

After getting off the bus one day, I noticed a bumper sticker on a parked car that said, "I've been to Graceland," or something like that. And I remember thinking, *"Graceland? Isn't that where Elvis lives? Lived?"* And that was my first conscious thought - the first time I thought of you as gone.

Sincerely,

Toni

10.

Dear Elvis,

After writing that last letter, I put my pen down and realized my granddaughter was standing behind me. "What are you doing?" she asked in her little girl's singsong voice which seemed to take it for granted she could ask me anything.

"I'm writing a letter."

"To Elvis?" My granddaughter's name is Chloe. She was six at the time and she had been reading for almost two years. And she knew who you were because she used to hear your music every time she came waltzing into my room, especially on Sunday mornings, which is when her mother likes to sleep late. Sunday morning is also when I turn on the radio to listen to Rockin' Ron Cade, a local disc jockey who has been playing your music on the oldies station every Sunday morning since - well, since you died.

"Yes," I told her, "I'm writing to Elvis."

"Why?"

"Well, since I lost my friend and I miss him, I thought it might help if I write to Elvis." Chloe didn't seem to think this was strange like I imagine most people might. She just nodded sagely and ran off to the kitchen as soon as she heard her father rattling some pots and pans. And, of course, she knew who I was talking about when I mentioned "my friend" since I had taken her to his house once to meet him when she was just a little bit younger.

We went on a summer afternoon and found him sitting beside the window in his TV room where the blinds were always halfway up. Chloe sat quietly for a while as Don and I talked, but she quickly became restless and we had to leave earlier than I had wanted to. We were on our way out of the TV room and were walking through the living room when I noticed she was looking at one of the two Christmas trees Don liked to keep up and decorated all year round. This particular tree was a four-foot table-top tree I'd given to him a couple of years earlier.

"Look Chloe, it's Christmas here every day and all year long," I said as I turned around to look at Don who was walking behind us. I reached up and put my arms around his neck. I smiled, and he smiled back. He held me tight for a moment before he released me. That was one of the last times I saw him. One of the last times I touched him.

Sincerely,

Toni

11.

Dear Elvis,

It was snowing that day, the day I heard about Don. It was the winter of 2013-14, the winter here when there didn't seemed to be any two days in a row when it wasn't snowing, about to be snowing, or hadn't already snowed. The storms began early that year. The first one came on a Sunday, the first of December, and when it came, it came without warning.

I was alone and sitting in a restaurant when it began. I had planned on that – on taking myself out to an early dinner and then to a movie. While waiting for my meal, I glanced outside and saw that an early morning rain had turned to snow, and that the snow was coming down so fast and furiously that within minutes the streets were covered.

A couple of people came into the restaurant telling everyone the roads were treacherous, so I decided to bag the movie and return home, which was the wrong decision. As it was, the drive, which normally takes less than twenty minutes, took close to two hours as I drove over slippery roads afraid, like everyone else, of sliding into the car in front of me.

It snowed three more times that month, and by the beginning of February there had been so many storms, I'd lost track of them. Most of them had come on weekends, often giving me Monday off and an extended weekend. Like those, this latest storm began on a Sunday, February 2nd. Predictions were that it would continue to snow all that day and throughout the following day. It was late that Sunday night when I got the call from my employer telling me to stay home and to stay safe on Monday.

I was happy about having the next day off even though I knew I'd probably get up early anyway and start writing. What I wanted was to write an epilogue for the book I had written. The book was a memoir about an attachment disorder I'd had as a child, and about how it had impacted the rest of my life, including all my adult relationships. The epilogue I wanted to write was to be about Don and the last time I saw him.

As soon as I opened my eyes that February morning, I could tell it was snowing. Looking toward the window I could see that the sky had that gray-white cast it always gets when it reflects the snow. At first I was too lazy and too comfortable to move, but then I changed my mind. Pushing back the covers, I got up and went to the window to watch the falling snow. Afterward I went into the kitchen to make coffee.

A few minutes later I was seated in front of my computer where I worked on the epilogue until mid-afternoon. When I was finished I was happy with what I had written. I felt as though I had gotten it right and as though the words said exactly what I wanted to express.

Here, in part, is the epilogue I wrote that day:

It was raining lightly as I pulled my school bus into the parking lot of the first school on my afternoon run. I was early and, because I was early, I decided to sit back and relax while I waited for my students to be dismissed. I closed my eyes and listened to the rain as my thoughts turned to Don.

I couldn't remember the last time I'd seen him - in the years since he'd retired from the school district there were sometimes weeks, sometimes months, before I saw him again. Once an entire year had passed before I saw him again and, although we had talked just a few days earlier, I wanted to talk to him again.

I picked up my cell phone to call him, but the call went straight to voicemail. His phone had never done that before. Usually it rang and he answered. I considered calling again, but the sound of children running toward the bus stopped me.

It was after four when I arrived back at the bus yard. I had decided I was going to go straight to Don's house, but changed my mind. I would stop at the club first. The club was the Knights of Columbus where he had been working since retiring from the school district.

As soon as I pulled into the parking lot, I saw his car tucked back in a corner. I went inside and stood for a moment while my eyes adjusted to the darkness. *There he is,* I thought when I saw him sitting alone at the far end of the bar, his eyes glued to the screen across the room.

"What are you doing here?" he asked, surprised to see me. I told him about the phone call. About how his phone had gone right to voicemail. I was worried. I was scared, is what I didn't tell him, but he must have heard the fear in my voice.

He smiled, told me he had turned his phone off on his way to his doctor's office and had forgotten to turn it on again. As he talked I realized I was standing too close to him, but I didn't move. I couldn't move. I stayed where I was.

"I wanted to see you anyway," I said. And as I smiled, he smiled too. We talked, caught up, and talked a little more until I realized I'd better get moving. But there was something I wanted to tell him, and although it was something important, I was having trouble finding the words. Later, I couldn't remember what words I'd used. Later, I could remember only that he had smiled as I spoke and then smiled again.

I remember that smile. I will always remember that smile.

Sincerely,

Toni
12.

Dear Elvis,

When I finished writing the first draft of the epilogue, I got up again and went to the window to look out at the snow. In Cindi's house, my bedroom was on the first floor and one of its walls was a sliding glass door that opened into a sunroom. Beyond the sunroom was the biggest backyard you've ever seen. (Oh, right. It may not be the biggest backyard you've ever seen, but it was big, Elvis. It really was.)

The snow was so incredibly beautiful it made me think of Don and I wondered what he was doing. He was home, of course, no doubt doing the same thing I was – watching the snow. Now wanting to connect with him again, I picked up my phone to call him, but got no answer.

"Where are you? Are you watching the snow?" I asked his voicemail. I could just picture him sitting in his rocking chair in the room where the blinds were always halfway up. He always sat there, watching the snowfall in winter, and in the spring he would be there again to watch the birds as they returned to his front yard.

Sincerely,

Toni

13.

Dear Elvis,

Of course, Don knew I was writing a memoir. He used to sit across from me in his TV room while I jotted down notes and ideas for scenes. My story started at the end of World War II when I was four and he was eleven.

"Do you remember the knifeman?" I asked him once, "The guy who used to go door-to-door to sharpen our knives?"

"For a penny," he said.

"Yes." I said, happy that he remembered. Happy that the knifeman had been real and not someone I'd just imagined.

"He wasn't the same guy," he said, and I laughed. Don and I had both grown up in Philadelphia, but in different neighborhoods; he in Germantown, I in North Philadelphia and later in West Oak Lane.

"How do you know that for sure?" I asked, and he laughed.

Sincerely,

Toni

14.

Dear Elvis,

After editing and completing the epilogue, I went into the kitchen for something to eat, which is why I didn't hear my phone when it rang. It wasn't until late on that snowy afternoon when I finally picked up my phone and noticed that a message had been left on my voicemail. I didn't recognize the number, but when I pushed the button to listen, I recognized the voice as belonging to Don's son.

On the phone, he sounded nervous. "Toni, this is Kevin. My number is," but he seemed to forget it. Remembering it again, he got through it. "Toni give me a call." After pausing for a moment he added, "I didn't want to do this in a message, but my father." The word "father" got caught in his throat and I hung up. I didn't want to know whatever it was he was going to tell me. I threw the phone across the room, and then wondering, *What if he's sick? What if he's in the hospital?* I picked it up again.

My whole body was shaking as I pushed the button to return his call. When he answered, I identified myself and he started talking. Somehow I knew what he was going to say even before he said it. I knew because Kevin was crying.

Later, I would wonder if I even responded. Later, all I wanted was to pick up the phone and call Don. I wanted to hear his voice, his laugh, his words. I wanted him *alive* again.

Later that night, in the middle of the night, I walked to the window. *Where are you?* I whispered. *Are you watching the snow?*

Sincerely,

Toni

15.

Dear Elvis,

Before getting back into bed I started rummaging around in drawers and cabinets looking for something to help me make it through the night. Eventually I found a half empty bottle of ZzzQuill and took a large dose. In the morning I awoke to the sound of snowplows and salt trucks as they slowly moved down our street. As soon as I could I got into my car and started driving. Believing that Don was lost somewhere out in the snow, I wanted to find him.

It wasn't until after noon when I finally pulled into the parking lot of a restaurant where Don and I used to meet for dinner. I went inside and had just ordered tea when an old song came over the sound system. That was one of the reasons we loved it there - because of all the old music that played in the background, although I wasn't expecting to hear this one. It was one of yours Elvis, your version of "Bridge over Troubled Water," and as I listened, I cried.

When the song ended I looked down and reached for my purse. When I looked up again a stranger was sitting across from me. At first, before I looked up fully and saw him completely, I saw only his wide chest and broad shoulders and, for an instant, I thought it was Don. But it wasn't. This man had sandy-brown hair (like yours was once), faded blue eyes, and a smile above his roman collar.

"I'm sorry if I startled you," he said. "I hope you don't mind. There are no other seats." He raised his hand to indicate the tables around us. I looked around then and saw immediately that the room, which had been empty a few minutes earlier, was now filled with people.

"Excuse me." I said. Embarrassed at the tears still running down my face, I got up and headed for the ladies room. Inside, I was sure I had imagined that man, but when I got back to the table he was still sitting there with a cup of coffee and a menu on the table in front of him.

"I hope you don't mind if I sit with you," he said. "It does get lonely eating alone all the time." Then, without waiting for an answer, he continued talking.

I learned that he was a priest who had just given a talk at a nearby seminary. He said he had left the seminary feeling famished and had decided to come to the restaurant for dinner. "I wasn't expecting company," he said. Which seemed, Elvis, like something I could have said too. I relaxed a little then and let him talk until he asked how long it had been since my friend died.

"How do you know about that?" I asked, looking up at his smiling face.

His smile disappeared. "You told me. Before you went to the ladies room. Don't you remember?"

But I didn't. He asked if I had anyone to talk to. When I told him I didn't, he said I could talk to him if I wanted to.

"But I thought you were a priest."

"I am," he said, "but priests listen," which hadn't always been my experience with priests. But there was something about this man that made me want to reconsider. "Besides, as a priest, I know something about death and grief." We continued talking until the waiter came and placed the check on the table between us.

"Thanks. I enjoyed your company," he said as we both reached for the check. He laughed then and I did too, the sound of my laughter surprising me.

It's all right. You're allowed to laugh," he said. "Listen, why don't we do this again? Next week. I'll even let you pay."

What could I say, Elvis? I smiled and nodded in agreement.

"You'd better get moving before the storm starts," he said. We were expecting yet another storm that night. This time the forecasters were predicting all ice. Deciding to take his advice, I thanked him and got up from the table. When I got to the door of the restaurant, I turned to wave goodbye, but he had already disappeared.

Sincerely,

Toni

16.

Dear Elvis,

What a voice you had Elvis! Of all the things I loved about you, what I loved the most was the sound of your voice. We were so lucky to have it for as long as we did and thanks to the miracle of recording, we will have it forever.

Just weeks before Don died I bought my first IPhone. After he died, I realized there was a recording of his voice in my voicemail. It was a message he had left for me on the 21st of January, just six days before he went to the hospital.

After listening to it once more, I went to an AT&T store and asked if there was some way I could preserve it, but they said no. They said it would be gone in a couple of weeks. Afterward I went home and found a locket my sister Joanne had given me. I put a picture of Don inside the locket and began wearing it, but oh how I wished there were some way I could put the sound of his voice inside that locket so I could hear it every time I opened it - or touched it.

Sincerely,

Toni

17.

Dear Elvis,

My friend Doreen posted a link on Facebook today. It was a link to a performance by you and Celine Dion on American Idol. The two of you were singing "If I Can Dream" and even though I have to admit that you looked kind of geeky in that white suit –which was perfect for 1968 – the producers of American Idol made you look great by putting all the Idol kids in white, too. Have you ever seen that Elvis? Have you ever seen yourself walking onstage in 2008 while the audience went wild? I saw it when it aired originally and it left me breathless.

    I know that in real life you performed that song only once, but you put so much into it that night that once was all you needed. I needed that tonight. I needed to "see" you again. You see, that's why I'm writing to you. Because like you, I too, have a dream and my dream is to see Don again. But that hasn't happened yet. Not even once. So you see Elvis, what I want is for him to come to me in a dream because like you I believe that if I can think, if I can talk, if I can stand, and if I can walk, then I can dream. And if I can dream, I will see him again. So please Elvis, make my wish come true. Now. Right now.

Sincerely,

Toni

Part 2

What Now My Love

In the night of death, hope sees a star, and listening love can hear the rustle of a wing.

Robert Ingersoll

18.

Dear Elvis,

I kept my promise and met that priest, Father Chris - he said his name was Father Chris - again the following week. When he asked if Don's death had been sudden, I told him it was. "At least it was for me. The last time I spoke to him was just a little over a week before he died and to me he seemed fine. I didn't even know he was sick. I didn't know when he was taken to the hospital. So yes, for me, it was sudden. Then, after he died, everything that happened seemed so surreal."

"What do you mean?"

"Well, after I left you I went home and started writing. I had no sooner put my pen down when the lights went out. Quite literally. I didn't know it at the time but, because of the ice storm, they were going out everywhere. All across the state. Then Don's son called to tell me the electricity was out at the Knights of Columbus where a luncheon was to be given in Don's honor, and that the luncheon was postponed until Friday." I stopped talking and looked down at the coffee in the cup in front of me. "Last week Father, I felt like a vagabond. When the lights went out at home, I went to Jessi's house, and when hers went out, I went to my sister Ginny's house.

"On Friday both my daughter and my sister went with me to the Knights of Columbus. When we got there the parking lot was filled with cars parked in every direction and in every possible space.

After we found a parking space, we walked in and my eyes went first to the far end of the bar where Don had been sitting the last time I saw him.

"It was strange being in that place without him. It felt as though I had reached the edge of reality. Somehow I made it through that event, but when it was over I felt as though I had been violated. I kept wishing there had been a service or something before the luncheon, but there wasn't.

"You see Father, Don didn't leave any instructions, and even though I think that was what he wanted, it wasn't what I wanted. Nor was it what I needed. I left wanting to find some place – a church perhaps – where I could light a candle and say a prayer." Eventually I found a place on line where I could light a candle. But a virtual candle isn't like a real one.

When Father Chris asked again if I had anyone to talk to, I shook my head. "Most of the people I know thought the relationship between Don and I ended long ago. Most people don't even know that I'm grieving.

"But I've been writing about it," I said, telling him how I'd been keeping a journal since I was a child, and how I had used it to write my memoir. But when he asked if I were willing to meet him again the following week, I hesitated. "Are you sure you won't have some priestly things you should be doing instead?"

He laughed. "I can arrange to do most of my priestly things and still find time to meet you."

Knowing I needed somebody to lean on, I agreed. "Okay," I said, "I'll meet you again next week, but when I do," I reminded him, "it will be your turn to pay."

Sincerely,

Toni

19.

Dear Elvis,

Two days later, on Valentine's Day, it began snowing lightly, reminding me of that first Valentine's Day after Don and I met when I gave him a poem that went like this:

It started
Barely noticeably,
Like a pebble
Tossed carelessly
Into a pond.

A word, a look.
Does he see?
Does he feel
The thousand tiny pins
That prick my skin?

I wait
As he becomes the ripple
That lines the bottom
And edges of my heart.
Does he see?
Does he feel?
I wait.

I didn't wait long did I, Elvis?

While running some errands that morning just after his death, I turned on the radio and heard one of your songs. It was "Can't

Help Falling in Love," and as I sat in my car listening, I felt Don's presence beside me. It felt so real, I reached out to touch him. Was it real, Elvis? Is anything real?

Sincerely,

Toni

20.

Dear Elvis,

I was backing my car out of the driveway one day in March when I noticed a cardinal fly past my windshield. The bird came so close that for a second I thought my car was about to strike him. But it didn't. I laughed then thinking he had really tried hard to make his presence known. But with other things on my mind, I soon forgot all about that bird until a few days later when my granddaughter came to my room and asked me to go outside with her.

The temperature was in the forties and there were still piles of snow littering the backyard, but the sun was shining as we grabbed our coats and headed outside. Chloe climbed onto a swing while I sat nearby, my eyes on the book I was reading.

"Mom-mom, did you see that?" she whispered a few minutes later.

"See what?" I asked as I looked up at her. "And why are you whispering?"

"I want to catch that bird," she said, pointing to a cardinal on the grass. Moving as stealthily as a six-year-old could, she began tiptoeing toward it, but the bird flew away before she could get closer. Disappointed, she headed back to her swing as I wondered if he had been the same bird I'd seen a day or two earlier. *Was the bird a sign?* I wondered, not sure I even believed in signs.

"Do you believe in signs?" I asked Father Chris the next time I saw him.

"Signs?"

"You know. From the Afterlife?"

"Do you?"

"Yes. No. I don't think so. Lately I've been having trouble believing in anything." I said as I looked up at the priest who was looking at me intently. "Father, I just want to go back to the way things were."

"You can't go back."

"I know, but I want to anyway."

"Are you angry?"

I shook my head.

"Are you sure you're not angry?"

"No. I'm not angry," I said, hearing the anger in my voice even as I said it. "Certainly not with Don."

"You're not?"

"No."

"You seem angry."

"If I am angry it's not with Don. It's," -I stopped.

"Tell me."

"It's with death. I'm angry with death," I said a little too loudly as people at the surrounding tables turned to look at us.

"You're angry with death?"

"Yes."

"But not with Don?"

"Okay. Okay. Maybe I am angry with Don, because he died. Why did he do that, Father? How could he die and not tell me first? And…and...?" I was fighting back tears now. "Who…who *told* him he could die?" I said as I picked up my cup and put it down again.

"Father, when Don was alive I used to say 'I love you. I always have. I always will.' But what I meant was that I loved him while we both were alive, and that I would love him again after we both had died. But what about now? What do I do now, now that one of us is dead and the other is not?"

"But you are loving him. Grieving is loving."

"Is it?" I asked shaking my head and looking at this man whose words I wanted to believe, but couldn't. "Father, I used to believe in love. I used to believe that love was the most powerful force in the universe, better than all of the powers the superheroes have. I thought that love could do anything."

"And it can't?"

I looked away.

"Tell me what love can't do?"

"It can't bring him back. It can't do that."

"Oh Sweetie, can't you see that there is no such thing as death?"

   But of course Elvis, there is.

Sincerely,

Toni

21.

Dear Elvis,

After Don died, I started reading books about death and dying, and books about life after death. One of the books I read was called *Answers about the Afterlife*, although God knows that at that point I was looking, not for answers, but for Don. The book was written by a man named Bob Olson, a private detective, who started looking for answers to his questions when his father died in 1997.

    I found Olson's book reassuring. Like Father Chris, Olson's book said that Don wasn't dead. It said he was alive, but in a form different from mine, and that the reason I couldn't see him was because his spirit vibrates at a level higher than mine.

    It said, too, that Don is nearby, that he is close, and that he can read my mind – read my thoughts – and if I want, I can speak to him *out loud*, as though he is in the room because, after all, he is. I read all of that one night and fell asleep feeling safe and feeling close to him.

    In the morning when I awoke, my eyes fell first on the space beside my bed, then on a white wicker chair at the foot of my bed. And then, looking at each, I asked *out loud:* "Are you here? Are you there?" And, feeling like someone from Dr. Seuss, "Are you anywhere?"

    Is he, Elvis? Are you? And what about God? Where is God, Elvis? I've been looking for him ever since Don left, but I can't find him either, and I'm afraid I'm running out of places to look.

Sincerely,

Toni

22.

Dear Elvis,

During the weeks and months after Don died I tried to stay busy. Actually, I had to stay busy. I had a book in production, and because it was a book I believed in, I wanted others to read it. But no one would ever even hear about it if I didn't learn how to market it.

So I was busy preparing myself for marketing, which wasn't easy because I was never like you. God knows I've never had your charisma, or your charm. Elvis, how did you get that way? How did you manage to charm the whole world almost overnight? Really, what was your secret? How could you be so gregarious when you were performing, and yet so shy when you weren't?

Come to think of it, in the beginning, not even you were sure how people were going to react to your music. After you recorded "That's All Right" and it was about to be played on the radio, you were so scared you went to a movie theater to hide. Little did you know what kind of reception your record was getting until your father found you and told you how the listeners of Dewey Phillips' "Red, Hot and Blue" show were demanding that he play it over and over again, and that Phillips wanted you to get to the studio so he could interview you. What a magical night that must have been for you!

How I loved watching you, Elvis. Even in the beginning. Especially in the beginning. There you were a kid from the South, who seemingly never even heard of segregation, blending all genres of music, crossing color lines and barriers to make music. God, you were so young, and yet you knew instinctively how to entertain people. You were so young and impulsive, and God knows you stayed that way, even after you became ELVIS. You were always young and impulsive. Always. Even until the end.

But if you were impulsive, Don was your opposite. I remember one of the last phone conversations we had together. It was just a couple of months before he died when, just after I said hello, he launched into a tirade. Politically he was a conservative. A right wing Republican, but he was a radical too. Extreme in his thinking, he would rant and rave about how the country was going down the tubes. And I, a diehard Democrat, would smile as I listened, amazed at the depth of his conviction, and at the extent of his passion.

Not that you weren't passionate. Anyone who listens to even just one of your recordings has to know that. When you sang we felt your passion. We felt your conviction. We felt what you were feeling.

Anyway, for me after Don died, all I wanted was to make the world go away. Even just the thought of standing up in front of a crowd of strangers was terrifying. I didn't want to entertain people. I wanted to stay at home. In my room. Alone. I wanted to write books. But I didn't want to write a book that no one had ever heard of, so I had to learn how to promote it.

At first it was easy. I started by going to book signings and presentations given by other writers, all of whom had different styles. Some were outgoing and gregarious, while others were quieter but still dynamic. I learned that book signings were easy because all I had to do was just show up and sign my name. But doing readings and presentations was going to take skills. Skills I didn't have.

As a child I had been diagnosed with rheumatic fever. The day before I was hospitalized I overheard the doctor talking to my mother. He told her I wouldn't have to go to the hospital if there was another place I could go where I could rest. A name was mentioned. A relative whose house was quieter than ours, someone who would have time to care for me, because at the time my mother couldn't or wouldn't.

That night, after the doctor told my mom I didn't have to go to the hospital, my father returned from work and I heard her tell him I *had* to go there.

Afterward I spent an entire year in that hospital lying in bed, feeling alone and almost never moving. I spent an entire year feeling abandoned and lost. When I finally returned home my oldest sister looked at me, amazed. "I thought you'd forgotten how to walk," she said. But I hadn't forgotten how to walk, I had forgotten how to talk. I had forgotten how to interact with other people.

On the advice of a marketing rep, I joined a group called Toastmasters International. The chapter I belonged to was a small group of about two dozen people who became my mentors and my supporters.

So I was busy all day, every day, and into the evening. But when I went home at night, it was grief that was waiting for me, ready to pounce on me as soon as I walked through the door. It was grief that came to me when I was feeling too tired and too vulnerable to resist it. Most of the time it came in the late evenings or in the middle of the night.

Sincerely,

Toni

23.

Dear Elvis,

One night when I was feeling more lost and alone than I had earlier, I turned on the TV and started watching a show my sister Ginny told me about, a show called Long Island Medium. Ginny said the medium was for real and that she could talk to the dead. So I turned it on and watched for a while, wondering if my sister was right, wondering if any of it was real, or if it all had been scripted. When I turned it on, the medium, whose name is Theresa, was telling someone that her loved one was always with her. "He is always guiding you," she said.

To me that sounded like Don. He was always trying to guide me, always giving me his best advice. Even though I didn't always take his advice, he was more often right than wrong and I always wound up wondering why I hadn't listened to him. So it made sense that Don would be trying to guide me now.

Then in early June, while I was driving through a neighboring town, I noticed a sign that read "Psychic Readings $10," and decided to stop. Inside the shop, I saw two chairs pulled up to a table covered with a deep blue cloth. Behind that was a curtain. I looked around the room which was empty until a woman with a headful of dark brown, almost black, curly hair and a pair of glasses hanging from a chain around her neck, opened the curtain and pulled up a chair.

"Hello," I said, but her mouth, obviously full, she said nothing.

"Are you a medium?" I asked. She stopped suddenly, midway between standing and placing her ample bottom onto the seat of the chair.

"No. I'm a small," she said sardonically.

"Oh," flustered, I tried to compose myself. "I meant are you a *psychic* medium?"

She looked at me. "Oh, do you mean can I speak to the dead? But of course." She waved her hand, indicating the empty chair. Then she stared into a crystal ball, while the room, which was already dark, grew darker. She closed her eyes and seemed to be praying. With her eyes still closed, she spoke. "The man you are looking for has just passed over. He wants you to stop worrying. He wants you to know that he is in heaven and that he is having a blast. A blast – that is his word. He is up there with his friends, all of whom got there before him."

She opened her eyes and stretched her hand across the table. I thought she was demanding payment, but I was wrong. Her voice became gentler and she smiled sweetly.

"Listen, Kid," she said. "If you want to hear from him, go home, sit quietly and do a white light meditation. Do you know what that is?"

I nodded, wondering how she had transformed herself so completely. One moment she seemed huge and intimidating and in the next, she was small and angelic. And why did she call me "kid" when I am at least thirty years older than she is? I paid then and left, hurrying away, already late for my meeting with Father Chris.

Time passed, but the sadness stayed with me. Sometimes when it rained I felt as though I were looking for Don between the raindrops, and when it was bright outside, I looked for him in sunlight. Father Chris and I continued to meet almost weekly until summer arrived and he said he was going away for a while. He said that although he couldn't give me an exact date, we would probably meet up again in September.

It wasn't until July when I finally remembered to look up Dolores Hart on the Internet, and when I did, I found her. She is a Prioress now at a Benedictine abbey in Connecticut. The abbey is called Regina Laudis, and it's the same one she entered in 1963.

In 2011, a documentary was made about her life. And guess what, Elvis? The documentary begins with a close up of your face, taken from the movie "Loving You." In it, you are singing a love song to Dolores. And guess what else, Elvis? Before Dolores entered the convent, she too, was in love with a man named Don. They were engaged to be married before she decided to enter the convent, and although he later dated other women, he never married. He used to visit her at the abbey, but he died late in 2011. In the documentary, there is a very touching scene between the two of them that made me cry.

At the beginning of the documentary Dolores says, "The abbey was like a grace of God that just entered my life unexpectedly. God was the vehicle." And then with a twinkle in her eye she adds, "He was the bigger Elvis."

I thought that was funny, Elvis, because back then we all knew God was bigger than you were. Even you knew that. Which is something most people don't know about you. They don't know how spiritual you were or how, even with all your fame and fortune, you were looking for more, for something bigger.

Sincerely,

Toni

24.

Dear Elvis,

When I first met Don I used to jump up every morning and run to work, but after he died I had trouble getting up and out of bed. When the alarm went off I would just lie there trying to think of some reason to get moving.

That summer when the school year ended, it got even harder, especially on the last day of the school year when I pulled my bus into the garage and backed it into its parking space. I turned off the ignition and surprised myself when I burst into tears. It wasn't until then that I realized how much doing my job had kept me feeling close to Don. On the road I looked for him constantly. Whenever I saw a car that looked like his, my first impulse was to follow it, hoping it would take me to where he was.

After that, getting out of bed seemed to take more energy than I had. Everything seemed to take more energy than I had, and sometimes – often – the day would seem to loom ahead of me as though it were a mountain too high for me to climb. By late August when I was feeling more lethargic than usual, I knew I had to find something to pull me away from my sadness, and I remembered how when I needed to feel energized, I would go on long walks.

There's a place in Philadelphia where I used to walk. It's a part of Fairmount Park called Forbidden Drive. As a child my father would take my sisters, my mother and me there and we would picnic in a grove on the other side of a long covered bridge that had a waterfall beneath it.

That part of Fairmount Park is so rugged it seems to have been untouched for centuries. Whenever I walked there as a child I believed if I could just turn around quickly enough I would see the Lenape Indians who hunted and fished and lived there long ago.

This area is so idyllic it has been immortalized in books by Mark Twain and Edgar Allen Poe, and has been used as a location in movies made by Brian de Palma and M. Night Shyamalan.

The trail, which stretches from the Chestnut Hill section of the city to within shouting distance of the Philadelphia Museum of Art, is studded with cedar trees whose branches seem to reach up into the clouds. Today it is still a perfect place to walk, or bike, or ride a horse (it is only automobiles that are forbidden here), although walking had not always been my forte.

I was forty the first time I tried to walk a mile. As a child, when I was hospitalized with rheumatic fever, the doctors told me I would never be able to participate in sports. But when I was forty-something and fiercely out of shape, my youngest daughter challenged and goaded me until I agreed to walk a mile with her. I wasn't too sure what I was in for, but as we drove to a nearby park with a mile long track, I reasoned it couldn't be all that bad.

We were two or three minutes into it when I started complaining. My daughter tried to distract me, but I wasn't falling for it. "Are you sure this is only a mile?" I asked after the first two minutes. She assured me it was just one mile around the track. I didn't believe her.

"This *can't* be just one mile," I said a minute later.

"No, Mom, it is." she told me again. Five minutes into it, I felt as though I'd been walking an hour.

"I don't think I'm going to make it," I told her two minutes later while searching for the end of the track. "Really, I can't make it. I can't go one step further."

"That's okay," she said cheerfully, "we'll just turn around and go back." I turned around then and happily, if unwittingly, walked the other half mile back to where we had started.

It was twenty years later, and just before I met Don, when I decided to try it again. I started slowly at first, a mile here and a mile there. And then more consistently. A mile a day and then two miles. Before I knew it, I was walking two, three or four miles a day. Then it was five, six or seven. One day I decided to try for ten. And I made it! Ten miles around the same track I had hated twenty years earlier. I was amazed. Ten miles took me three hours and twenty minutes. But I loved it, every step of it. It felt so good *being athletic*!

Sometimes I'd break it up into shorter walks, occasionally along Forbidden Drive. As I walked, I fell in love with the weather and taught myself to tune in to the nuances of the day, those subtle but inevitable changes that came with each hour. When it rained, I had the park all to myself, alone with my umbrella. Unfortunately, I had fallen out of that habit and, by the time Don died, I walked for exercise only occasionally. Now I needed to start walking again.

I was on such a walk in September when I saw a familiar figure walking ahead of me on Forbidden Drive. It was a man walking slowly, slowly enough for me to catch up with him. When I did, I saw that it was Father Chris.

He seemed as surprised to see me as I was to see him. We talked about his summer and about his plans for the fall, but when he asked how I had been doing since the last time I saw him, I shook my head. "Father," I said, "I keep wondering what Don knew and when he knew it. I was trying to remember what we had talked about during our last conversation, on January 22. Then I remembered how crazy that week had been for me, filled with too much snow and too many trips over slippery roads.

"Monday was Martin Luther King Jr.'s birthday, and because a storm was predicted for the next day, I left home and went to Jessi's house so I would be closer to work when it started. On Tuesday the snow was so heavy I had no sooner taken my students to school when I had to turn around and deliver them back home again.

"I remember standing in front of the large picture window in Jessi's living room late Tuesday evening looking out at the snow. As usual it reminded me of Don and I tried to reach him. When he didn't answer, I left a message.

"'What's wrong,' he asked when he returned my call.

"'Nothing,' I told him, 'I just wanted to hear your voice.'"

"'Oh, I thought someone had died,'" he responded.

"On the phone that night he sounded good to me, but he also sounded restless. *Probably from being indoors,* I'd thought.

"At one point during the conversation he said, 'My feet are going numb. They say the feet are the first to go.'" I shook my head. "*Go where?* I'd thought, not making a connection. Now I keep wondering what he knew and when he knew it. Did he know he was dying? And if he had, why hadn't he told me?

"When I tried to remember what I'd been doing five days later when he was taken to the hospital, I remembered going to work that Monday morning and noticing how unbelievably high the snow was, piled on every street corner and in every parking lot. As I drove away from work after my first run, a chill ran through me, and I felt almost compelled to call Don, but it was early and I knew he'd still be sleeping. Instead I drove by his house. But when everything looked normal, I kept on driving.

"Why hadn't I stopped? Why hadn't I followed my impulse and knocked on his door? Later, when I went back over the events of that morning, I remembered hearing a siren. During the luncheon, after his death, a friend of his told me Don had called him to ask for a ride to his doctor's office. His friend said he took one look at Don and told him they were going straight to the emergency room.

"After he told me that, I couldn't help wondering if that was the siren I heard. I couldn't help wondering why Don hadn't called me."

"If he had, what would you have done?"

"I would have gone there. I could have." -I stopped.

"What? Do you think you could have saved him?"

"*Seen* him. I could have seen him again."

"Maybe he didn't want you to see him like that."

"Like what?"

"Dying," he said and then he added, almost to himself, "You seem to be moving backward instead of going forward."

I can't go forward. "Father, why do people die? Why did Don have to die?'

Father stopped walking. Turning to look at me, he asked, "Toni, have you ever been in the hospital? Have you ever been in pain?"

"Yes," I said as we continued walking. "About a year ago, I had a gall bladder attack. I was in so much pain, I couldn't watch television. I couldn't read. I couldn't do anything. I just wanted to," -again, I stopped.

"What?"

"Die."

"Toni, Don was in pain. Terrible pain. His heart was failing. His body was failing and he couldn't take much more." By now I was crying. Father led me to a park bench and took my hand in his. "God took him. Toni, the body dies when it's had enough. The body dies, but the soul does not."

"Never?"

"Not ever."

"Are you sure?"

"I am absolutely positive."

"Listen," he said. We had continued walking and were close to the lot where we had parked our cars. "There's a restaurant around the corner. Bruno's. Do you know it?"

"Yes."

"Why don't you meet me there?"

Sincerely,

Toni

25.

Dear Elvis,

I arrived at Bruno's a few minutes later and saw that Father was the only person sitting on the deck outside. As I sat down across from him, he told me he'd ordered for both of us. I smiled. When he asked me to tell him about my other experiences with grief, I told him how it had been cold and snowing back in 1987 when my father died.

"It was another February day, cold and brutal as the snow fell in large, heavy clumps that quickly covered the streets and lawns around my parents' house. By the time the storm ended, two days later, there were more than thirty inches of snow on the ground.

"My mother, my sisters and I were all gathered around when my father lapsed into a coma. Worried about driving over snow-covered roads and slippery railroad tracks, and about the teenage children I had left at home, I decided to leave. I arrived home safely, took a shower, and had a hair dryer in my hand when the telephone rang. It was my younger sister, Joanne, calling to tell me our father had passed.

"What if I had stayed? I wondered irrationally. *Would he still be alive? How is it,* I wondered later, *that we believe that making different choices or living differently is the antidote for death?*

"But I managed to hold myself together and go on – at least until the funeral. During the viewing the night before, I'd looked at him - at what was left of him after death and disease were done with him - and thought, *This is not my father.* I hadn't realized I'd spoken out loud, but I must have because I felt Joanne's hand on mine. 'I'm so glad you said that,' she said.

"The next day as Mass ended, the organist began playing a hymn that describes how a soul reaches heaven – "On Eagles

Wings" - and I started to cry. *You have to be there, God,* I thought as, even in church, I wanted to raise my fist to God. *You **have** to be there. You promised."* I stopped talking for a second and looked up at the sky, and then back at Father Chris. I sighed.

"Then twenty-six years later, and one year before Don died, it was February again. But this time there was a hint of spring and it was almost warm. This time it was my sister who was dying.

"Joanne and I hadn't been close, not since we were children. Maybe not even then. I hadn't seen her in years, not until her husband died and I went to the funeral. We reconnected and hung on to one another. Looking back later I saw that we had been clinging to one another for dear life. We went out to dinner together. We went on vacation together. We even watched television together. Then one day she told me she'd been falling down. 'Just falling down for no reason.' She told me when I asked.

"'There has to be a reason,' I said. But she insisted there was none. She'd seen two doctors. She'd had tests done, but they found nothing. Then one day she fell down the steps at our youngest sister's house. It was Christmas Day. She went to the emergency room the following day.

"She was lying in a bed when a doctor walked up to her and said, 'You have stage 4b lung cancer, small cell. You have one week left to live.' Either that was exactly what happened or, in her shock, that was what she heard.

"Seven weeks later she lay dying in a bed in her daughter's house where heavy curtains covered the windows to block out the sunlight and to keep it from hurting her eyes. I wanted to do something – anything, but there was nothing I could do. I closed my eyes and listened to her breathing. Moments earlier her son-in-law was in the room with me. We were waiting for the hospice nurse to arrive. Joanne awoke suddenly and Mark jumped to his feet. 'What's wrong?' he asked.

"'Get Stephanie,' Joanne said. 'Hurry.' When Stephanie came into the room asking what was wrong, Joanne said 'the nurse is here.'

"'No, not yet,' Stephanie said. 'He'll be here in twenty minutes.' Joanne looked confused. Stephanie left the room saying she would be back in a few minutes. I got up and stood beside Joanne.

"'Did you see the nurse come in?' she asked.

"'No,' I had to tell her. She looked upset and unsettled.

"'Are you all right?'

"'I can't wait twenty minutes,' she answered.

"'Close your eyes. The time will go more quickly,' I told her, hoping she would sleep. She closed her eyes, and her breathing deepened as I sat down beside her, wishing there was something I could do for her.

"'Do you think there's a heaven?' she had asked me two weeks earlier.

"'I am absolutely sure of it,' I had answered.

"That time I was certain. That time I knew there was a God. I never doubted it. I believed in heaven. There was no need to threaten or to demand that God show himself. He showed himself anyway as I looked down at my sister and saw that there was a picture of an eagle on the blanket that covered her.

"So I wasn't there when my Father died," I told Father Chris. "Earlier that day I remembered how he always said the two of us, both he and I, had been born on a Tuesday. When I left his house that day, I was sure he was going to survive. *People born on Tuesdays don't die on Sundays,* I'd thought. Death laughed when it heard me think that. It laughed *out loud* because death doesn't play by the rules. Death doesn't have any rules. It seems that death can come for anyone at any time.

"When I discovered my mother had Alzheimer's, her illness put me off. I took it personally, as though she had contracted it as one more way to keep me at arm's length the way I believed she had since I was a child. But as time passed and I watched as little by little she started disappearing inside herself, my compassion grew and I was able to reach out to connect with her in ways I was unable to as a child.

"But I wasn't there when she died, despite the fact that one of my sisters called to tell me she was dying. I got angry. *How does she know?* I wondered. *She's just telling me that to get a rise out of me the way she's been getting a rise out of me ever since we were kids.* So I didn't go until it was too late.

"And I wasn't there when Joanne died either. I knew she was dying, and I ran. She'd been staying with her daughter, just outside of D.C., and I drove down to see her. To be with her. But in the end, I couldn't face it. I couldn't let her go, or stand by and watch her go. So I ran. I'm still running away from death. I'm still running as fast as I can," I said as I closed my eyes. "And I wasn't there when Don died either."

"What would you have done if you had seen him before he died?" he asked.

I opened my eyes. "I wouldn't have run," I told him. "I wouldn't have run the way I did with my sister. I know I would have stayed. Not to watch him die, but to beg him to stay. But I never got that chance. Nor was I given a chance to say goodbye."

"Do you still believe in God?" Father asked; and, even though he spoke gently, I got angry.

"Yes, I still believe in God. But," -I stopped.

"Tell me."

"I still believe in God, but believing in him and trusting him are two different things."

"Trusting him with what?"

"Oh, you know," I said sarcastically, "with the little things. Like life itself."

"Maybe that's because our lives aren't meant for us to keep."

"It seems there is a whole long list of things we aren't meant to keep."

"Like what?"

"Like everything!" I said. Again I was speaking too loudly and again, heads began to turn. I was silent for a moment and then, "Listen, Father, before I met Don, falling in love wasn't something I expected to happen. It was definitely not something I had been planning on doing. I'd been there. I'd done that. When I fell in love the first time, I had been so deeply and passionately in love I thought nothing could end it until one day when God laughed at me.

"'Ha,' he said. 'You think you're so much in love! You think you're so committed! Take this.' And, like a grenade, he threw divorce at me and all that love, all that passion, exploded in front of me, leaving me alone until I met Don.

"And after I met Don, I thought, *What, God? You want me to do it again? Is that what you want? Well, I won't do it, God! It's not what I want. Leave me alone. Don't ask me to fall in love again.* But he doesn't always play fair, our God, does he Father?"

I took a deep breath. My knuckles were gripping the edges of the table. There were tears in my eyes, but I ignored them. "So I fell in love with Don even though I felt he wasn't willing to fall in love either.

"But I did fall in love with him until one day when I thought, *Stop, I can't do this anymore. I can't love him any more than I do.*

And God laughed at me. 'Ha,' he said, 'you think you're so in love? You think you're so committed? Take this.' And this time he threw death at me. Why did he do it, Father? Why did he give me a mountain this time?"

Sincerely,

Toni

26.

Dear Elvis,

When Father Chris asked if I really believed God sent me a mountain, I nodded.

"Then climb it," he urged. "You can do it. I know you can."
"You sound just like Don."
"Don? Don told you that?"
"Yes."
"When?"
"Recently."
"What?"
"Father, I have a confession to make."

He looked at me strangely, but said nothing as I told him about the medium I had visited. "In fact there were two mediums. I found the second online and called her. As soon as she spoke, she said a male spirit had stepped forward and that his first name began with the letter 'D.'

"Right away she had my attention. She asked if I had a question for him and I said I wanted to know why, if he and I were so close, he left without telling me."

"And what did she say?"

"She said he was hesitant at first, but that he knew I would be all right. I kind of laughed at that, wondering how Don could possibly know I would be all right."

Father smiled. "What else did she say?"

"I asked him why, if we were close, I hadn't been with him in the end and she said that he had wanted to see no one at the end, and that he wanted to keep his leaving private. She said that despite this we were close and that his feelings for me had never changed, that they were what they were from the beginning, but that in the beginning he had problems – and then she named some of the problems – some of the medical problems I knew he had.

"She said he stepped back because he didn't want to burden me and when he stepped back, he was sad and unhappy, but that he did it because he felt he had to protect me. Then she said he was still protecting me and always would."

"And did you believe what she told you?"

I shrugged.

Father Chris smiled again and told me to keep moving forward. "Keep moving forward until you get to the top of that mountain."

"That's what the medium said. She said Don wanted me to keep moving forward. But what if I don't want to climb that mountain?"

"Climb it," he urged.

I looked away.

"No. Don't look away. He believes in you and he wants you to believe in yourself."

"But all I want is to see him again."

"Climb that mountain," he whispered as he picked up the check the waitress had placed on the table between us. He started to get up from the table, then changed his mind. "By the way, did you know that Elvis once recorded a song called *Padre*?"

"Yes. It was one of his favorite songs."

"Mine too."

"Really, Father? You're a fan?"

He smiled. "Oh, and did you know that a blind man once climbed Mt. Everest?"

I looked at him dubiously.

"It's true. You can look it up on that computer of yours."

Sincerely,

Toni

27.

Dear Elvis,

An old song got stuck in my head late one day until finally I stopped singing it long enough to wonder if you had ever recorded it. It was an old Rogers and Hammerstein song from the 1940s called "If I Loved You." When I went to the computer I found you singing it on YouTube and, as I listened, I got goose bumps.

Of course, you must know what people say about goose bumps? They say you get them when the spirit of the person you are thinking about runs through you. Is that what happened Elvis? I don't know. Maybe it is.

What I do know is that I was happy when God sent me someone to love. But now I'm stymied. Now I feel as though the love is still here, not in my heart, but in my arms and it is so heavy I can't carry it any longer. Tell me Elvis, why did he send me someone to love and then take him away?

After Don died I was consumed with thoughts about death and dying. Before that, the only other time I can remember worrying about death was when my ex-husband was in Vietnam. Then, I thought about death all the time. Night and day. Asleep and awake. It was always on my mind.

And it didn't help much when I saw that picture – when I got up one morning and walked downstairs to make coffee. I opened the front door and picked up the newspaper and there it was on the front page - the picture of the South Vietnamese officer holding his arm outstretched and pointing a gun at the head of a Vietcong prisoner.

When I saw that picture and the look on the face of the man about to be shot, everything went white – me, the room I was in, even the newspaper I was holding. After that I worried even more about death until somebody finally said Nathan wouldn't die in Vietnam unless there was a bullet with his name on it. Then I worried about bullets – bullets with names etched on their casings.

Now, at night, I wake up to the sound of his name ringing over and over again. *Don...Don...Don,* like the sound of a bell inside my mind. *Don...Don...Don,* like a question unanswered.

Within months of his death, I began finding it difficult to remember his face. I could recall parts of his face, parts of his body - his hair, the tip of his nose, his arms, even his belly, but I couldn't put them together. I couldn't remember the face I once thought I had memorized. But that other face – the one I saw for only an instant, and only as the result of the flash of a camera – is etched forever in my mind.

One night while I was lying in bed trying to remember his face, I thought instead of that other face. *What was his name?* I wondered? *Didn't that prisoner have a name?* But I did not ask his name out loud. I dared not ask for whom the bell tolled when I knew it tolled for Don.

Sincerely,

Toni

28.

Dear Elvis,

Grief, the intensity of grief, comes and it goes. It changes and it remains the same. In his book, *A Grief Observed*, C. S. Lewis wrote "no one ever told me that grief felt like fear." And in her memoir, *The Year of Magical Thinking,* Joan Didion wrote about her grief over the loss of her husband: "Grief turns out to be a place none of us knows until we reach it…We might expect if the death is sudden to feel shock. We do not expect this shock to be obliterative, dislocating to both body and mind."

For me, because there was no funeral and no service either, grieving was difficult. As I went looking for Don, day after day, grief felt like some perverted form of a child's game of Hide and Seek. "Come out. Come out wherever you are" my heart called and my mind screamed.

There were days after his death when I felt as though I existed in some other dimension, some other place where people could see me and hear me, but couldn't touch me. Nor could I touch them. Hearing about his death made me feel as though I were falling into a deep, dark space. All I wanted then was to close my eyes and to sleep, but I was afraid of closing my eyes, afraid that if I were to open them again, I would look up and see that someone was closing the lid.

And then there were moments when I no longer feared death or what it could do to me. It was as if, in those moments, his death had inoculated me against worrying about my own.

Father Chris told me again that there is no such thing as death and that I could still keep loving Don, but I didn't know how. "When he died I wasn't ready to say goodbye," I told him. "When my mother died she came to me in a dream that night, or the next, but I have yet to see Don, and I can't help wondering why he won't come to me in a dream."

"Maybe he's waiting."

"Waiting for what?" I asked.

"For you to come away from the deepest part of your grief."

When I got home that night I fell into bed exhausted. Unable to sleep, I picked up one of the two books sitting on my nightstand. It was one of Elizabeth Kubler Ross' books on death and dying, one in which she writes about a man who lost a leg during a near death experience and then talks about having it in heaven.

I rubbed my eyes. *But what,* I wondered, *was he standing on?* Could it be possible that nonphysical existence is the real thing and that what we are experiencing here is nothing more than a reflection of that reality? Is heaven real and earth imagined? Or is earth real and heaven imagined? Perhaps both are real. Or maybe one is the mirror image of the other. In the other book, *The Holographic Universe*, I found something that seemed to back up that last thought.

In its introduction, author Michael Talbot writes that he believes in the paradigm which states that the world "and everything in it – from snowflakes to maple trees to falling stars and spinning electrons – are also only ghostly images, projections from a level of reality so beyond our own it is literally beyond both space and time."

Exhausted, I put the books down and closed my eyes, realizing it had been one of those days when I felt as though I had been crying all day and as though I had been trying to see through walls, to see through matter and to look at spirit. And even though I was beginning to believe that Don was here, that he was nearby, I still wanted to *see* him.

That night in a dream I found myself walking along a street in an unfamiliar neighborhood. I was alone at first until I realized both sides of the street were lined with houses and that people were pouring out of them. Suddenly there were hundreds of people walking with me, all of us walking in the same direction. Most of the others were walking more quickly than me.

As they passed, I looked at their faces hoping to see someone I knew. I kept walking, wondering where they were going, but I didn't stop to ask. I just kept walking. Finally, I saw a woman I knew, who had just left her house and was walking with a young boy.

Are you going too? She asked when she recognized me. She and the boy had already gone past me, but she was looking at me over her shoulder. *Where are you going?* I asked? *Are you going to a concert?* Suddenly I want it to be a concert. I want to hear music. *No,* she yelled back. *It's a graduation. Come with us.*

She pointed up ahead to where I could see a stage with a curtain that was closed. I decided to join them, then changed my mind when I realized the street we had been walking along – the one I thought was so wide and endless – had narrowed and become a dead end. Somehow knowing these people were moving toward death, I turned and started running away, still looking at the faces around me. Still looking for someone I knew. But I couldn't find him and when I woke up I was alone again.

Sincerely,

Toni

29.

Dear Elvis,

I was feeling down early one Sunday morning when I decided to turn on the radio. Rockin' Ron's show was on and he was playing one of your songs, "Are You Lonesome Tonight." It was the version where you mess up the words and start laughing right in the middle of the recording. Then you sing a word or two more and burst out laughing all over again, and continue laughing all the way through to the end of the recording. As I listened, pretty soon I was laughing too.

Like you, Don was full of fun and loved to play. About a week after our first date together, Jessi invited him over for game night. Don and I were seated at her dining room table, destroying her and her kids at Trivial Pursuit, when Don said something that made me laugh.

"My mother laughs at everything you say," Jessi said, looking only at Don. Indignantly, I denied it even though I had just been laughing.

"Yes, she does. She would laugh if you said the alphabet," she said as I rolled my eyes and Don just sat there looking amused.

"Say it," she said.

And like an idiot, he did. "A, b, c," he began, and I fell over laughing.

Sincerely,

Toni

30.

Dear Elvis,

I just realized I never told you about the second time I fell in love with you, which by the way, was the topic of discussion between Father Chris and me one day just before Christmas.

"Father, there's something I've been meaning to tell you."

"Go on," he said when I hesitated.

"Okay, well, do you remember when I told you that after I met you, I went home and started writing in my journal?"

Father nodded.

"And do you remember how I told you I had no sooner finished when because of the storm the lights went out?"

Again, he nodded.

"Okay, well, later that night, in the middle of the night, I got up and started writing again, this time by candlelight. But it wasn't until the next morning when I picked up my journal that I noticed I had begun writing 'Dear Elvis' instead of 'Dear Dov.'" I looked down at the table and at the coffee in my cup. "Father," I asked, "do you think that's crazy?"

Father shook his head. "What I think," he said, "is that you were probably in shock after hearing about Don. But why Elvis?" he asked as I began telling him the story I'm about to tell you.

It was 1992 when it began. By then, my kids were grown and living on their own, and I was alone - and lonely. Although in those days I didn't admit to that, not even to myself. I just went along as best I could ignoring all the evidence but looking, definitely looking, for something – for anything - to fill the big empty space I felt deep inside myself. And then one night I sat down to watch a movie.

It was the movie about you taken from the book Priscilla wrote about your relationship. Elvis, that wasn't even you on my TV screen, but some other actor playing your part, and yet I was enchanted. The next day, I started looking for everything I could find out about you. I bought every book ever written about you, listened to every song you ever recorded, watched every movie you made, and every movie made about you.

This searching took a long time, weeks turned into months and then it became more than a year. My enchantment became an obsession, but it was a sweet obsession. The whole time I was searching, I knew I was on a path and I knew the path was taking me somewhere, but I didn't know where. Furthermore, I didn't even care. I was enjoying the journey.

And then one day my searching ended. There were no more books to read. No new songs to wait for. And when I was finished I felt as though I knew *nothing* about you. There was more. There had to be more because the big empty space that had filled up when I was searching was empty again and I was lonely again.

After I found everything I could about you, I started haunting all the bookstores near my home, but I found nothing more about you. Then one day I decided to drive all the way to the Northeast section of Philadelphia because there was a bookstore on Cottman Avenue near Roosevelt Boulevard that I wanted to check.

I don't know if you remember, but in those days there was no Amazon and no Barnes & Noble stores like there are today. There were just tiny little mom and pop stores with narrow aisles and shelves full of books that went up to the ceiling, and whenever I stood inside one of those stores, I could feel all the knowledge surrounding me. Sometimes I could almost believe that if I were to try hard enough, I could absorb it all - like osmosis - through my skin.

At first I didn't see anything about you in that store and I was about to give up when I finally saw a small paperback book with your name on it. I didn't even look at its title, and I barely noticed that the picture of you on its cover was really kind of ghostly looking. I just grabbed it, paid my $3.95 plus tax, and raced back home to read it.

As it turned out, that little book was the last one I read about you. It was the last one because when I finished it, I felt as though I knew all I needed to know about you.

When I got home from the bookstore I pulled the book out and looked at its title: *Elvis after Life.* I read that and suddenly I didn't feel so good. I figured it was going to be a collection of stories like the ones in the National Enquirer, stories about a bunch of people who thought you were still alive and living in Kalamazoo or Timbuktu, or wherever they thought they'd seen you or wished they'd seen you.

Then I read the subtitle: *Unusual Psychic Experiences surrounding the Death of a Superstar.* I blinked and read the subtitle again. I turned the book over and read the back cover: "Intensely moving, unforgettable accounts by people whose lives were touched by Elvis - after his death!"

After his death? Unbelievable! I thought, but I sat down and started reading it anyway.

Elvis, there were stories in that book about people who said they had premonitions about your death, and stories about people who said they saw you after you died. There was one story in that book about a woman, a professional psychologist, who believed you appeared to her as an apparition. She said she interacted with you, that you sat across from her at her desk and talked to her about where her life was going.

Then there was the story about a policeman whose son had run away. In a dream you told the father you wanted to help him because his son was a fan of yours. You told him you were worried because the boy had fallen in with the wrong people and was experimenting with drugs.

Don't ask me why, but I believed that story. Mostly I guess because it sounded like you, like who you were in real life - the generous and caring human being who was always buying cars and houses for people, sometimes even for people you'd met only once.

In the dream, you showed that policeman a map of a city he wasn't familiar with. With your finger you pointed on the map, showing him landmarks. You made sure he was paying attention so that when he went looking for his son, he would find him exactly where you said he would be. Which is exactly what happened.

By the time I finished that book I felt so close to you, Elvis. It wasn't anything weird. I mean, I didn't have apparitions or even dreams or anything. I didn't believe you came to me in dreams. I just felt connected to you in a way I couldn't understand, but trusted. There were just simple things like waking up one day and feeling an urge to turn on the radio, knowing that when I did I would hear your voice. And when I turned it on, I did.

Years later, when I tried to understand what had happened to me back then, I picked up a copy of the biography Peter Guralnick wrote about you, *Last Train from Memphis.* In it, he quotes Sam Phillips as saying that when he discovered you, he saw something in you "to mirror his own self-image" and that you - in combination with "the elements of the soil, the sky, even the wind, the quiet nights, the people living on the plantations, never out of debt, hoping to eat" - represented all of the things that made this country great.

"And Elvis Presley," Phillips continued, "may not have been able to verbalize all that - but he damn sure wasn't dumb, and he damn sure was intuitive, and he damn sure had an appreciation for the total spirituality of the human experience.'

In his book, Guralnick concluded that that was your mark - that you conveyed your "spirituality without being able, or needing to express it. And all these adults with their more complicated lives and dreams and passions and hopes were looking for themselves in your simplicity." And that was me, Elvis, because the second time I fell in love with you, what I fell in love with was your spirit.

Sincerely,

Toni

31.

Dear Elvis,

When I finished telling Father Chris all that I just told you, I told him how after reading *Elvis after Life,* I had checked out its author and learned he was a pioneer in the study of near death experiences. "His name was Dr. Raymond Moody and he had written another book called,"

"*Life after Life,*" Father interjected.

"Yes. Do you know it?"

Father nodded and I continued. "So it was back to the bookstore I went to buy a copy of that book which talked about people who'd had near death experiences, and about life after death.

"But it wasn't Dr. Moody or even his books that led me back to God. It was Elvis. Like him, I started meditating and turning inward until I found that quiet sacred place inside myself. But after Don died, I felt paralyzed. I was afraid of turning inside, afraid that turning inward would mean turning toward more loss and pain. Instead I turned to Elvis and started writing to him." Again I asked him if he thought that was crazy.

"What I think is that for you - with your history and fascination for Elvis - turning to him must have felt natural."

"It did feel natural. It does feel natural."

"Tell me, when you write to Elvis, what do you write about?'

"Mostly I write about my feelings. And I ask him a lot of questions."

"What kind of questions?"

"I ask him about his life here on earth and what it's like in heaven. I ask him about God and about the afterlife."

"And do you expect an answer?"

"No. Certainly not a letter, but I expect," -I hesitated, "something."

"Like what?"

"I'm not sure. Just – something." I said as I looked down at the coffee in my cup. "Father, I wish," I said, but then I stopped.

"Tell me what you wish."

"I wish Don could appear in front of me and sit across from me the way Elvis sat across from that psychologist in the book I read."

"That isn't going to happen you know. When your resolutions come, they will come in your mind."

In my mind? I thought, knowing my mind was too busy dealing with death to be dealing with resolutions.

"Tell me," he said, "what it is you need to assuage your grief."

I just looked at him.

"Humor me," he said. "Pretend I'm a genie."

I tried to smile but the effort fell flat. "Father, I want to see him again. Even if it's just in a dream. Even if it's for just five more minutes. I want him to have the service he never had. And I want him to have the funeral he deserved."

"Okay," Father said, and I blinked.

Sincerely,

Toni

32.

Dear Elvis,

I was paging through an old journal not long after Don died when I found an entry about a dream I had almost a year before his death. In the dream I was standing outside a concert hall waiting for him so we could go inside together. It was almost time for the concert to begin and I wanted to go inside, but I couldn't because he had my ticket.

I kept scanning the faces of everyone walking passed me, but none of them was his. Finally, I saw him, but when I did, he walked right passed me. And he wasn't alone. He was with his wife, the woman he had been married to for almost forty years, the woman who had died five years before we met.

I watched as they went through the door and then I turned around. But as I headed home, I thought that maybe if I went back and stood outside I could hear the one song I wanted so badly to hear even though in that part of the dream the song had yet to be identified.

When I returned, it must have been intermission because people were standing around in small groups of two or three. I went up to one of them and asked if the song I wanted to hear had been performed yet. Oddly, I couldn't remember the name of the song, but I remembered a couple of the words and I began to sing them as softly as I could.

Then, in my dream, I heard the song in its entirety, and when I woke up I could still hear it. The song was "Someone to Watch over Me," and even though I can't remember who it was who recorded the original version, in my dream I heard every word of it being sung as though it were a mini concert being performed just for me.

When I found that entry in my journal the other day, I couldn't help wondering if the dream had been some kind of premonition and that I had known, even then, that Don would be leaving soon, going someplace where he couldn't take me, and that I had been looking - somewhere in the recesses of my mind - to comprehend his leaving, and to see it as a place where he might somehow watch over me.

Sincerely,

Toni

33.

Dear Elvis,

I remember reading in one of the books I found about you years ago that you were never very good with money. With handling it, that is.

You really didn't have a clue, did you Elvis? I remember reading too, a book that said you always kept a one million dollar balance in your checking account. Now who does that?

I also read more recently that you never carried cash. Not even loose change. Which made me laugh because you and I are so similar in that I always spend money as though I have a million dollars to back me up, but in my checking account I never seem to have any more than what amounts to loose change.

Don, however was so good with money that I found it easy to picture him growing up in the 1940's. As a child, I'll bet that if he had three pennies he would have managed to save two of them and to spend just one. Which is not at all the situation with me. As a child, if I had three pennies I would have spent all three of them and wound up in debt after borrowing another from one of my sisters.

The first time Don and I had a conversation about money was just after the Christmas holidays. I didn't work during the holidays and, therefore, I didn't get paid. "Things will get better as soon as your cash flow gets started again," he said when I complained about having to wait a couple more weeks for a full paycheck.

I had never heard anyone use the words "cash flow" in a sentence before, nor had I ever seen those words used anywhere except in a textbook, so when I heard Don use them in relation to me, I laughed.

"My cash doesn't flow," I told him. "It may have trickled once or twice, but it's never flowed." Now it was his turn to laugh.

But he tried. Oh, how he tried to channel me into someone who could save money. I just never seemed to be able to do it. Oh, I could put a couple of dollars away every once in a while, but then some emergency or another would arise and I would have to use it.

Besides, I didn't have a very good attitude toward money. I used to work in a bank and money always seemed – well, kind of dirty. Eventually however Don did get me to see its usefulness, but having the ability to save it continued to elude me.

Elvis, I was telling Father Chris all this during lunch one day. I was telling him how when Don died, my finances were in their usual disarray. "I was about to give up on them entirely when it occurred to me to ask Don for help. I asked him to be my patron saint of finances." Father smiled and I continued, telling him how I had applied for a loan and was really surprised the next day when it was granted.

But before long I was in trouble again, so I told him to forget it. I told him not to worry about my finances, but instead, to help me on the road because even though I work only part time now, I am still on the road twenty to twenty-five hours a week. So I asked him to protect me when I was driving.

A day or two later was Halloween and I wanted to see Chloe dressed in her costume. It was after 4:30 by the time I got off work and, because of daylight saving time, it would soon be dark. So I decided to drive the quickest way possible which involved taking the turnpike.

There I was on the Pennsylvania turnpike driving eighty-five miles an hour in the fastest lane when the car to my right started moving toward my car and into my lane. I quickly swerved to the left to avoid being hit and almost struck the concrete barrier which was there to keep me from moving into oncoming traffic.

When I swerved to the left, I almost lost control of my car and of course, I had to swing back again to the right, again a little too quickly, and again the car zigzagged almost hitting the car that was still moving into my lane. Petrified and not knowing what to do, I lifted my hands from the steering wheel. Miraculously, my car straightened out and continued down the highway. As soon as I could, I moved to the middle lane and stayed there, deciding that going sixty miles an hour in the middle lane was good enough for me.

"So what do you think, Father?" I asked when I finished telling my story. "Do you think that was Don who took the wheel when I let go of it?"

"Maybe," he said, "maybe it was Don. But from what you've said, I think your finances may be more out of control than your car ever was, and that it may be a better idea for you to go back to asking him for help with your money."

Sincerely,

Toni

34.

Dear Elvis,

My daughter came home from church one Sunday in October and sat at the dining room table drinking tea. She wanted me to join her. She wanted me to sit with her so she could tell me about some event she was planning. I sat down beside her and tried to listen, but I was too easily distracted.

There was a church bulletin sitting on the table between us. My eyes were drawn to two words printed on it. "Grief Programs," I read. "There will be workshops to explore new and meaningful ways to explore your grief. All are welcome," it said. "RSVP."

I called the next morning and spoke to a woman named Dolores who said the workshops would be held on three consecutive Sunday afternoons in November, ending just before Thanksgiving. I told her I'd be there. I thought it was a good idea. I thought it would be a good place to talk about my grief. When I told Father Chris he said he thought it was a good idea, too.

In the meantime I got a call from a friend of mine named Mike, who had lost his son a couple of months after Don died. Mike called to tell me about a special Mass of Remembrance that was going to be held at his church, which was also the church closest to where Don lived. I wasn't sure if Don was a member of that church, but I decided to find out.

When I called a woman answered. I told her about Don. "I don't know if he was a member, but he lived nearby."

"But the mass is only for members of the parish who died during the past year," she said.

"Oh," I responded as I started to cry. "He may not have been a member," I continued, "but he was raised Catholic and he belonged to the Knights of Columbus. When he died, there was no mass," I said. "And no funeral either."

She told me to hold for on a minute and I heard her talking to someone in the background. "It's okay," she said when she returned. "Your friend will be included in the Remembrance. Will you be attending the mass?"

"Yes."

"Good," she said. She asked for his name and wrote it down. She said a candle would be placed on the altar with his name on it. "You can take it home with you, but his name won't be on the program. I'm afraid they've already been sent to the printers." I thanked her and hung up, promising to be there.

A week later, I arrived at the church and saw two dozen candles all lit up and lining the foot of the altar. A candle with Don's name was among them. I took a seat and picked up a program surprised to see that his name had been included. *They must have called the printer in time,* I thought.

When my friend and his wife, Debbie, arrived the three of us sat together. It was a beautiful mass, sad but comforting the way a requiem mass was meant to be. Afterward, I said goodbye to my friends and went to the door of the church where several people were standing, blocking my exit. I heard them exclaiming. After they moved, I stood at the doorway of the church and saw what they had seen - that it was snowing and that large heavy flakes were falling through the sky.

Snow in November is so rare in this area that when I saw it I smiled. As I walked from the church I saw that the snow had already covered the parking lot and all of the surrounding landscape. As I watched, the snowflakes kept changing. At first they were thick, heavy and beautiful as they fell in clumps all around me. Driving home I felt as though I were riding inside a snow globe. But, despite the falling snow – or maybe because of it

– I found myself smiling.   Just before I got home the snowflakes thinned out, and with the light reflected on my windshield, they looked more like raindrops – or tear drops.

Finally, I pulled into the driveway and got out of my car as they changed again, looking now as though they were light and weightless as they fell onto my outstretched hands and disappeared.

When I got into bed that night I finally felt as though I would fall quickly and easily to sleep, even as I wished once more that Don would come to me in a dream. Just before falling asleep I thought about the theme of the priest's homily, which in one word could be summed up as "Believe," and I remembered how, on the previous night, I had gone to a local theater to hear an author talk about his latest book. Both of my daughters and two of my granddaughters had gone with me to hear him. Afterward, when I asked him to sign my copy of his book, I asked him to wish me good luck with the memoir I'd written. "Good luck with your book," he wrote and then he wrote just one more word. In large lopping letters he wrote the word "Believe."

Sincerely,

Toni

35.

Dear Elvis,

I was late for the first meeting of the grief group. After punching the address into my GPS I chose a route going north on Bethlehem Pike instead of south. When I finally found the right place I realized the meetings were being held inside a funeral home. *People never go to funeral homes willingly,* I thought. *Unless they have to.* Emotionally, I had to.

As I pulled into the parking lot I realized the old stone building fit in perfectly with the surrounding neighborhood, a neighborhood I had driven through hundreds of times while driving my school bus, and that the building was located just a block away from Lindenwold Castle, which is also known as St. Mary's Villa. The castle, along with most of the homes in the area, had been built by a pharmaceutical industrialist in the early 1900s and would later become the site where the movie *The Trouble with Angels* was filmed.

I went inside the funeral parlor and started looking for the meeting, peeking into rooms I was afraid of peeking into. By the time I found the meeting and took a seat at the table almost everyone else had spoken, describing their loss. When it was my turn I told them I had lost a friend. As I described him, the tears I'd been holding back began to flow. I let them flow. Here they could flow. Here everyone cried. It was safe to cry here.

The conference room we met in was large and all fifteen members of the group, including the two women who led it, had suffered a loss. Most were recent. In the past year. Most of the members were grieving the loss of a spouse. Some were mourning a child. I was the only one who had lost "a friend."

One of the women leading our group gave us a sheet of paper containing a list of thirty emotions related to grief, and asked us to circle the ones we felt pertained to us. I circled all but five of them.

Within minutes, I realized our group included an entire family - parents mourning the loss of a child, a young woman mourning the loss of her sister. Their grief, deep and intense, seemed to fill the room. Another member of the group, a man with white hair and a face that seemed to age as he spoke, told us how his wife of fifty-two years, "a woman who had never been sick a day in her life," fell to the kitchen floor one day and died. "She was just…gone," he stammered. "How do I deal with that?"

I knew what he meant. How is someone so alive one moment and gone the next? Completely and irreversibly absent. Elvis, why is death so merciless?

Sincerely,

Toni

36.

Dear Elvis,

When I returned to the grief group the following week I realized it felt good to see the other members of our group. It was as though we were old friends, friends with whom we had shared something precious and rare. Without them I would not have been in touch with my sadness, and I *had* to be in touch with my sadness.

During the meetings tears ran down my face like raindrops on a windowpane. Before the meetings, I felt as though I were wearing a deep heavy cloak like those worn by the women in Afghanistan. Like them, my eyes were covered and I could see nothing except through an onerous veil of sadness and sorrow.

During the last meeting one of the men said he had begun making it a practice of doing something every day to honor the memory of his loved one. After thinking about it, I decided to put Don's picture and the votive candle I'd gotten at Mass on the mantle beside my bed. At a craft store I found a miniature rocking chair just like the one he sat in every evening and placed it next to his picture. Feeling prepared, I started to get ready for the holidays.

At midnight on Christmas Eve all the hustle and bustle seemed to dissipate. A hush fell over me as I thought of you, Elvis, and wondered if up in heaven every day wasn't just like Christmas.

Down here, Christmas day came with all its usual magic and miracles - and still, I cried.

Sincerely,

Toni

37.

Dear Elvis,

When Father Chris asked why dreams are so important to me, I told him it was because I once had a dream that saved my life and the life of my grandson. It happened on Christmas Eve in 1996 just weeks after I moved into the mother-in-law suite in Jessi's house.

On the evening of the twenty-third my oldest grandchild, Michael, who was eleven at the time, decided to throw a party for his friends from middle school. When the party ended, Michael was invited to spend the night at the home of one of his guests.

Jessi's husband was a truck driver, and earlier that day he had taken their two youngest boys over the road with him so Jessi could finish her shopping, wrapping, and the other preparations she needed to complete before she could start to cook our Christmas Eve Feast of the Seven Fish. That Christmas Eve tradition had been celebrated in our family for as long as I could remember, first by my mother and then by my daughters. When I was a child the entrees included calamari (squid), scungilli (conch), baccala (cod), anchovy pasta sauce, smelts and shrimp. Although it was originally meant to be a penitential meal, my daughters took the word "feast" a little too literally and liked to add things like caviar and lobster.

The house we were living in was shaped like an "L." Most of the time we entered through the basement door from the back driveway where the two lengths of the "L" met, and where we parked our cars. The mother-in-law suite was in the basement, and just outside of it was a set of stairs. At the top of the stairs was a hallway. To its left were three bedrooms, and to the right was the rest of the L-shaped house - the living room, kitchen, dining room and beyond that, the master bedroom.

It was just after midnight when the telephone rang. The caller was the father of Michael's friend who told Jessi that Michael had gotten up, and was holding his head and screaming. Jessi woke me and asked me to go with her to get Michael. She wanted to take him to the emergency room. On the way, we took the youngest child, Tori, to stay with Jessi's mother-in-law.

When we returned from the hospital it was almost time for me to get up and get ready for work. Exhausted, I decided to call out, which was something I did rarely and was reluctant to do then. At the time I was still working at a bank, and I knew it would be busy on Christmas Eve. After calling, I climbed back into bed and did a brief meditation. Feeling more relaxed, I drifted easily into a peaceful sleep until suddenly I heard a voice urging me to get up.

Someone was calling my name, over and over again, saying, *Toni get up. It's time to get up.* I opened my eyes and looked around, but there was no one else in the room. No one urging me to get up. I decided I must have been dreaming. I looked at the clock beside my bed and saw that it was 11:07. *It can't be that late,* I thought still feeling exhausted.

I had only recently moved into the mother-in-law suite and its bathroom was still incomplete. Because of that, I used the bathroom upstairs. I got up that morning, pulled on my robe and walked through the kitchen where I glanced at the clock on the wall. (It was the clock Cindi had given me a year earlier, a clock that depicted you, Elvis, wearing a blue-checked suit and blue suede shoes on legs that swung perennially back and forth like a pendulum.)

I opened the door to the apartment and started walking up the stairs, which is when I heard a sound I'd never heard before. It was a hissing noise just above my head, coming from where the upstairs kitchen was located. I reached the top of the stairs, pushed the door open, and saw nothing in front of me except dark vicious clouds of smoke.

At first I couldn't comprehend what I was seeing. When I realized what it meant, fear wrapped itself around me and I started screaming. Michael, who was trapped in his bedroom, heard my voice and responded. I told him to come toward me. I told him not to be afraid, but to just keep moving toward the sound of my voice. I heard his door open. He rushed toward me. I told him to go downstairs, out the back door and to the neighbor's house. "Tell them to call the fire department," I said.

In the meantime I was screaming for Jessi and Tori. In my mind I could picture two-year old Tori with her hair, long and curly, and dressed in a nightgown as she toddled down the hallway the night before. I remembered that when we returned from the hospital Jessi said she was going to sleep in Tori's room which was next to Michael's, and even closer to the fire than his.

Why couldn't they hear me? Why weren't they answering? Had the smoke already overcome Jessi? Had it overcome Tori's little lungs? I looked again to my right and saw the smoke moving like angry clouds across the living room toward the front door. I turned and ran back down the stairs, grabbed my cell phone, dropped it and picked it up again. By now I was beyond hysteria. I ran back up the stairs and called for Jessi again. Just then Michael returned.

"Don't come back up," I told him. I ran down the stairs to join him, and together we ran out the back door and around to front of the house where we heard the fire engines racing toward the house.

I don't remember much of what happened during the next few hours, although I do remember the firemen going back inside the burning house three times before I finally accepted the possibility that Jessi and Tori weren't in there. With Michael and several firemen behind me, I ran around to the back of the house. It was then that I saw what I had not seen earlier – Jessi's car was gone. Her parking space was empty.

A few moments later, after Michael and I returned to the front of the house, I realized Cindi and her husband were standing beside me watching as the firemen put out the fire. I realized I must have called her earlier and she had made the twenty-minute drive from her house in what seemed like seconds.

When the fire was out an inspector told us it had started in the dishwasher which Jessi had started before she and Tori left the house that morning. Later while we were clearing out the debris left after the fire, I picked up the clock that had been hanging on the wall in the upstairs kitchen where the fire started and saw that it had melted during the hottest part of the fire. Looking at its hands, I saw that it had stopped at exactly 11:07.

Sincerely,

Toni

38.

Dear Elvis,

Shortly after the first anniversary of Don's death, I turned to Father Chris and asked him again why people have to die. "I mean, what's the point of living if we just have to die anyway."

"Maybe that isn't the question you should be asking. Maybe the question is why are we born?"

I closed my eyes, then opened them again. "When you said that Father, it reminded me of what I learned as a child. It was the first, or maybe the second, thing I memorized in school. It was a question from the Baltimore Catechism, 'Why did God make me?'"

"And do you remember the answer?"

"Yes. 'He made me to know him and to love him in this world and to be happy with him in the next.'" I stopped to add sugar to the cup of coffee on the table in front of me. Then I continued. "Isn't it funny the way that's worded? I mean, there's no mention of being happy in this world?"

"No, it only mentions 'knowing and loving God in this world.'"

"But how is that done?" I asked, "It seems to me that between the two, between knowing and loving, and being happy, the first is the bigger mystery. And maybe that's why we set our sights on 'happy.'"

"Before you met Don, were you happy?"

"No, but neither was I unhappy. I was content."

"And after you met him, were you content?"

"No. Not at all. I wanted more. I always wanted more."

"And so in the end what did you wind up with?"

"In the end Father, I wound up knowing and learning a whole lot of things I never would have if I'd never met him, which are all of the things I put into my memoir."

"So maybe that's the answer to why we are born. We are born to learn."

"So then why do we die?"

"Why, to be happy of course."

I sighed "If only it were the other way around," I said.

Elvis, are you happy? Somehow I think you are. Even happier than you were here on earth when you were standing onstage singing your heart out. Even though I know you are probably happier in heaven, somehow I wish you were still here with us.

Sincerely,

Toni

39.

Dear Elvis,

When I was a child growing up in Philadelphia, my father took my sisters and me to see the movie *The Great Caruso* because our last name was Caruso and because he said we were somehow distantly related to the Italian opera singer, Enrico Caruso. But, after seeing the movie, it wasn't Caruso I was drawn to, but the actor who portrayed him, Mario Lanza. I was intrigued in part because like me, Mario Lanza grew up in Philadelphia. He was our very own Italian tenor, one whose greatness inspired later tenors like Luciano Pavarotti, and whose voice matched yours in that he had a range of between two and three octaves.

Elvis, like you, Lanza died prematurely, and under unusual circumstances. He was only 38 and a patient at a clinic in Rome where he was put to sleep for prolonged periods of time in order to induce the weight loss required before making his next movie. At the time I knew none of this. After his death, I spent a lot of time looking for a biography of his life, but I was never able to find one. What I was looking for was verification of something I had read in the newspaper. It was an article about Mario Lanza's widow which said she died shortly after he did. It said that she died of a broken heart.

A broken heart? Do people really die of a broken heart? I wondered back then. I wanted to verify that, but I could never find it verified anywhere else. And since I was only eighteen when she died, maybe I thought dying of a broken heart was somehow romantic.

Do you remember when I told you about watching the documentary *God is the Bigger Elvis*? Well, after I watched it, I decided to read Mother Dolores' memoir *The Ear of the Heart*.

And Elvis, can you guess what I learned? In her book she says the very first telephone call she received in the convent was from you, telling her you were praying for her.

And guess what else I learned? She was related by marriage to Mario Lanza. Her father's sister, her Aunt Betty, was Mario Lanza's wife. As I was reading her book, I kind of held my breath waiting for her to verify that her aunt's death was caused by a broken heart. Although she writes about how devoted Betty was to Mario, she never mentions how she died.

Then one day when I got to my literature class early and was waiting for it to begin, another student, a woman named Rochelle, came up to me and asked if I were the one who wrote the memoir.

When I told her I was, she told me she was writing one too, and that hers was about becoming a widow. She and her husband had been married for fifty-three years. "We were kids together," she said. Then she told me how, after his death, she had been hospitalized and was diagnosed with something called Takotsubo, a Japanese word for an illness known as "the broken heart syndrome." Finally, I found the verification I had been seeking.

"When Don died did you think you were dying of a broken heart?" Father Chris asked when I told him about meeting Rochelle.

"No, not the way she was. Not in any physical way. But I do think that dying of a broken heart happens much more often than we think it does."

"Really?"

"Yes. And I believe it happens just as often to men as it does to women. You see Father, I believe that's how Elvis died, too."

"Elvis?"

I was looking down when he replied. Looking up quickly I caught his smile, but as quickly as I noticed it, it disappeared.

"And you don't think it was because of the drug abuse?"

"No. Not really. I mean, of course the abuse contributed, but even today's forensic pathologists are divided on what caused his death. Anyway, for me, I believe he died because his heart was breaking.

"But doesn't broken heart syndrome usually happen after the death of a loved one?"

"Usually, but not always. According to the American Heart Association, it can happen after a betrayal, and God knows Elvis believed he was being betrayed by two of the bodyguards he had known since high school, the ones who wrote a book about his addiction to prescription medication. He was worried about what his fans would think of him. But most of all he was worried about what Lisa Marie would think and believe about her father.

"Father, have you ever heard Elvis sing "Hurt"? There's a music critic, Dave Marsh, who said that after he heard it for the first time, he couldn't help thinking that if Elvis felt the way he sounded when he recorded that song, it's a wonder he managed to live as long as he did."

"Well, you seem to know more about it than I do."

"Only what I've read."

"Of course."

"Father, what you did a minute ago, Don used to do that."

"Do what?"

"That smile. Don used to smile at me like that whenever he liked something I was saying or doing or just because, well, just because I was there. He did it all of the time at first, but then after the romantic relationship between us ended, he'd tried to hide it. If he saw me noticing, off would come the smile and up would go the mask just as if he were Jekyll and Hyde, but a sweeter version, of course."

"And speaking about a breaking heart. Father, do you know what the last thing is that Don said to me? On the phone that day I was thanking him for something he had done for me and when I finished he said something that startled me. He said 'I'm glad I did something right.' It broke my heart when he said that because he had done many things right but didn't seem to know it.

"Anyway, I'm glad I got a chance to thank him. And I want to thank you, too, Father," I said as I picked up the check and looked for my wallet. "You've helped me a lot, brought me through a lot during the past months."

"Here let me," he said taking the check from me.

"Thank you," I said again. "Father, there is something I'd like to do now. I want to go on a retreat. To Regina Laudis."

"To Regina Laudis?"

"Yes."

Father shook his head. "Actually," he said, "I have a better idea."

"Better than a retreat?"

"For you? Right now? Yes."

Did you know about this, Elvis? No, of course not. How could you have known what Father Chris was thinking?

Sincerely,

Toni

Part 3

The Impossible Dream

I have dreamt in my life, dreams that have stayed with me ever after, and changed my ideas; they have gone through and through me, like wine through water, and altered the color of my mind.

Emily Bronte

40.

Dear Elvis,

It was less than a week after that meeting with Father Chris. My daughter and her husband had been vacationing in England, but I was expecting them to return momentarily. Jessi was no sooner in the door when she began talking about her trip, and she continued talking about it until late into the evening.

She was clearly enthralled, so I listened patiently – or as patiently as I could until I found a way to escape and run off to bed. But in the morning she began again until I saw clearly there would be no stopping her unless I could come up with a way to distract her. Which is exactly when I decided to ask her.

"Do you want to go to Graceland?" Despite the fact that it was Father Chris' idea, going to Graceland was a trip Jessi and I had been talking about making for the last twenty years.

"Now?" my daughter asked.

"Yes."

"Sure." Then she, who was already packed asked, "How long will it take you to get ready?"

"About an hour." And so it began, as we left an hour later – even though it was already well passed two in the afternoon.

It was exhilarating driving toward your home in Tennessee. I was glad Jessi was with me, especially since she insisted on doing all the driving. On the way, she listened to country music stations that kept fading in and out as we progressed, while I read one of the books assigned for the literature/discussion class I was taking.

We drove straight through, stopping for a late dinner that first night in a town called Bristol, which was just north of the Virginia - Tennessee border. Our waitress turned out to be an exchange student from England. You would have thought my daughter and she were long lost friends as they began chatting away about merry ole England, a place to which they both clearly longed to return.

Later we stopped at a hotel. We got up early the next morning, driving until we reached Memphis in the late afternoon. It was, at that point, too late to visit Graceland, but I wanted to at least drive passed it. When we arrived at 3764 Elvis Presley Boulevard, I looked at the music gates and then beyond them at the expansive lawn, but I didn't see Graceland.

"Turn around," I told my daughter, "I didn't see the house. I want to see the house." We turned around and I caught my breath when I saw it standing at the top of the hill and to the left, looking like a photograph come to life.

We drove on then, heading to Sun Studio, which was filled with memorabilia from your life and career. By the time we got through all the exhibits and entered the recording studio, I was already feeling saturated.

It was awesome being in the recording studio that many have called the birthplace of rock and roll. Inside that room, I felt as though I could almost hear the voices of you, Johnny Cash, Jerry Lee Lewis and Carl Perkins as you rapped and jammed your way through *The Million Dollar Quartet.*

For me the most awesome moment was standing by the front door - the very place where your career began. I couldn't help wondering how you must have felt the first time you entered that room. How excited you must have been. You had so much to look forward to – the possibility of being discovered must have been like reaching out and touching the golden ring on a carousel.

Later, on our way to Beale Street for a late dinner, we made a turn and suddenly there it was stretched out in front of us - Ole Man River - the Mississippi in all its glory, with the Hernando de Soto Bridge all lit up and looking more beautiful than a Christmas tree.

We left bright and early the next morning for Graceland. We parked across the street, then boarded a bus that took us to the music gates and through them - where I felt like Alice moving through the looking glass. Slowly the bus moved up the hill and to the back of the mansion, where we unloaded, and where for a moment I felt as though I had come home.

The path to the front of the mansion is on a slight incline, and I could see at least a dozen other people ahead of us, one of whom looked familiar. For a second I thought it was Father Chris, but whoever it was disappeared inside the house before I could get closer.

I stepped through the front door of the house and realized right away that I was looking, not for Father Chris, but for you, Elvis, my eyes going first to the top of the stairs, then to the right and into the living room with its fifteen-foot sofa and the baby grand piano in the music room beyond it.

As we walked through the rooms, I realized I was looking for you everywhere, in the dining room where you sat at the far end of the table, in the jungle room, and in the racquet ball building. I even looked for you in the lounge, where I saw a piano and could almost hear you singing what was reported to be the last song you sang, "Unchained Melody."

I looked in your dad's office and by Lisa Marie's swings. I looked everywhere, but I couldn't find you. Oh, there were images of you. There were images and pictures of you everywhere, all throughout Graceland and throughout Memphis, too. But I couldn't find YOU, Elvis. I couldn't find your spirit or any sign from your spirit the way I had been hoping to.

Despite all this I loved Graceland. I loved its ambiance and its spaciousness. Elvis, people are always asking me which of your songs I love the best, and that is such a difficult question to answer. Besides there are so many that I love, it always seems to depend on my mood, or the weather, or the time of day before I can answer that question truthfully. There is however, a trilogy – no not "An American Trilogy" – but a trilogy of songs you performed and recorded near the end of your life that I've always loved best, "Hurt," "Danny Boy" and "Unchained Melody." I don't know anyone who doesn't love those songs, especially "Unchained Melody."

A long time ago when I was married, Nathan told me that if he saw a little boy standing on a street corner singing that song, and even if he were singing it off key, he would stop to listen. Anyway, as I was standing by your grave inside your meditation garden I couldn't help thinking of the words to "Danny Boy," and I thought my heart would break because you are no longer with us.

As I walked through the grounds of the estate, I was wearing headphones and listening to a tour guide. My favorite part of the tour was listening to Lisa Marie talk about how excited she always became whenever she saw you make your entrance on stage. She said it didn't matter that she had been with you five minutes earlier, because when you walked on stage you were somehow transformed into someone magical, almost mystical. Listening to that, I could almost feel your presence beside me. Almost.

Sincerely,

Toni

41.

Dear Elvis,

When I returned from Graceland and started telling Father Chris about my trip, he looked dismayed. "So you didn't find what you were looking for?" he asked.

"I didn't say that. I didn't find what I was looking for in Memphis, but we had a good time. Getting there was exhausting. And so many things went wrong. We weren't in Memphis for more than an hour when we got caught in a downpour just outside Sun Studio. We were soaked to the skin. Then Jessi got a speeding ticket for going *forty-five* miles an hour on a highway, and the hotel we booked, sight unseen, was just about the most God–awful place on earth."

"Still, you had a great time?"

I smiled. "Yes. We spent hours and hours at Graceland visiting every shop and every exhibit despite its being more hot and humid in Memphis than I imagined it would be. We had burgers and fries for lunch, but later when I found a restaurant that offered fried peanut butter and banana sandwiches, I had to try one although I had recently read a book by one of Elvis' maids who said she never knew him to have one. I had one and I loved it."

Father smiled and I continued.

After leaving Graceland, we went back to the motel, which we had picked from Jessi's iPhone. The night before, after signing in and getting our keys, we walked through the door of the room and were met with the overpowering smell of perfume. "I don't like this," Jessi said, "It makes me wonder what they're covering up." The place smelled like a bordello. Exhausted from traveling, we stayed the night.

Tired now from the tour of Graceland and the Memphis heat, we decided to rest before going out again. This time we went to the Lorraine Motel, where I stood on the pavement looking up at the spot where Martin Luther King Jr. was shot in 1968. Standing there, I thought about the speech he had given the day before he died, the one in which he talked about reaching the mountaintop.

Outside, the motel looked like any other, but inside there was a huge atrium. Amazed at its size, I spoke a little too loudly. "Wow, Dr. King got shot in a nicer motel than the one we slept in last night," I exclaimed as everyone standing near us laughed.

The motel, which is now the National Civil Rights Museum, was packed with information and exhibits about events that had filled the headlines during my early twenties, but the most poignant moment came when I looked at the open bathroom window from which Dr. King was shot. Later, we left the museum and went again to Beale Street for dinner.

The next morning I asked Jessi to drive to Humes High School, the Lauderdale Courts and to the house you owned on Audubon Drive. I didn't want to miss anything or any opportunity to find what I was looking for, even if I didn't know exactly what it was I was hoping to see. We even looked for the rooming house you lived in when you first moved to Memphis. Finally, just before noon, we headed for Tupelo.

I loved Tupelo. I really did. I loved its small town atmosphere and its streets, which seemed somehow newer and less dusty than those in Memphis. In Tupelo we stopped for lunch, shopped at the hardware store where your mom bought your first guitar, and walked through the fairgrounds where you gave your homecoming concert in 1956. Finally, we headed for the two-room house your daddy built before you were born.

We were standing on the front porch near the swing when I told Jessi the story your daddy told you about your birth, about the loss of your twin brother Jesse Garon and how, when he stepped outside after you were born, he saw a blue light in the sky hovering directly above your house.

We walked through the house and then to the church next door. A tour guide explained that the church, which was the one you sang in as a child, had been moved to this site after you died, when a larger church was built for the congregation.

Inside we sat in a pew - maybe one you sat in once - and watched a short film, then exited by a side door. Deep in thought, I was looking down as we left the church, but Jessi was looking up.

"Mom, did you see that?" she said suddenly.

"See what?" I asked as I looked up at her. Then, trying to be funny, I added, "Did you see a blue light?"

"It was a bird," she said. "A cardinal. It flew into that tree."

"Where?"

"Right there," she said pointing to a branch. I looked at the tree, which stood midway between the church and the house, and watched as a bright red cardinal lifted its wings and flew from one branch to another.

Sincerely,

Toni

42.

Dear Elvis,

In the documentary, *God is the Bigger Elvis*, there is a scene in which a man comes to the convent to visit Mother Dolores, who welcomes him by name and seems to know him.

"How can I help you?" she asks.

"I have been looking for Angelina," he answers. "And I haven't found her."

"You will," she assures him as I sit there stunned. *The woman is lost? Has he been to the police? Why doesn't she tell him to report Angelina as missing?* I wonder until I realize Angelina has died and this man has been looking for her, much as I have been looking for Don.

In a voiceover, Mother Dolores says, "I think people come to speak to us about every possible form of suffering that hits the human heart. My role is to help a person to discover you can always find hope. And if you can find hope, you might find faith."

When I went to Tupelo and saw that little bird I found hope, but I had yet to find faith. Faith didn't come until later. Dear Elvis, there was a day when my grief was at its most severe, a day when Father Chris asked me what I needed to assuage my grief. I told him what I needed was to give to Don both the service and the funeral he deserved, and to see him again, even for just five more minutes. The first, of course, happened when I attended that Mass with my friend Mike and his wife Debbie back in November. The second happened after I returned from Graceland and sat in front of my computer to watch your funeral.

I watched for a long time as the sixteen white limousines moved from Graceland, through the city and into the cemetery, and as the thousands and thousands of people who lined the streets, mourned you. As I watched – and I hope you don't mind too much – in my mind I pretended that funeral was for Don, and finally I felt at peace with his death. My third wish came true when I saw Don in my dreams.

The first time I saw him I was standing outside his bedroom window, except in the dream it was a screen door instead of a window. I was getting ready to knock when I saw him inside, making his bed. "Hey, Sexy," I said, "Can I come in?" As I spoke he looked up and, seeing me, he smiled. He put the sheet down and walked toward the door. And, as he opened it, I awoke - ecstatic at finally having seen him and his smiling face.

A few nights after I had that dream, I had another. This time I dreamt we were lying in bed together. In the dream I was lying on top of him. With my head on his chest, I was listening to the sound of his heartbeat, feeling the rise and fall of his breathing. I laid there a moment or two, then lifted my head. We kissed and I returned my head to his chest. Awake, I realized I was lying on my stomach still feeling the warmth of his body beneath mine. I continued to lie there for another moment or two, until finally I moved and the dream faded.

Not long after returning from Graceland, I went to visit my son who lives in Germany. While there we took a train to Bad Nauheim, where you were living while serving in the Army. I saw the house where you and Priscilla met. I ate at the bakery where the cake for your twenty-fourth birthday was made. I even had a slice of that chocolate cake – they still make it, using the same recipe. Then Eric and I walked up the hill and through the town, and he took a picture of me standing at the exact spot where a picture of you in uniform was taken for the cover of "Soldier Boy."

During all this time and afterwards I continued to see Don in my dreams. But, of course, even then there were days when I felt as though grief had returned to assault me. There were days when I felt like a child lying on the floor kicking and screaming, "I want him back. I want him back."

And then one night I dreamt I was walking through my living room when I heard a knock on the door. The door opened and I saw Don standing there with a suitcase in one hand and an overnight bag in the other. I watched as he swung his arm back and tossed the overnight bag into the room. Looking at him, I could tell he was angry, angrier than he'd ever been before. And, without even one word spoken, I knew why.

I watched as he took a step forward, and then I woke up. Awake, I felt lost and confused until, remembering the dream, I laughed and whispered into the darkness, "It's okay Sweetie. You don't have to leave heaven. I believe."

Seeing him in my dreams, I just can't help believing.

Elvis, do you remember giving a speech in which you said that as a child you were a dreamer, a little boy who read comic books? A little boy who became the hero in the comic books? You *were* a hero Elvis, for me and for so many others.

Dear Elvis, I have heard that like the eyes, the voice is a doorway to the soul. If that is true then yours is an enormous soul. Marion Keisker was right, you know. If we loved you (we did, and we do) it was because in looking at you, we saw ourselves.

So, thank you Elvis, for the music you gave us, because down here it is music that gives us wings. And thank you for listening. These letters have been where I have put my sadness – and my joy. But joy cannot be contained. It is not in joy's nature to be contained. Therefore, my letters will stop now, as they must stop, except for my one last, very special letter - to Don.

Thank you, Elvis. Thank you very much.

Sincerely,

Toni

Dear Don,

I didn't want you to die. I wasn't expecting that. Not so soon. Not without warning. I was hoping we would get back together again. Not romantically maybe, but together again – at least for a little while, and I thought if we did, I'd get it right this time.

There were days right after you died when I was angry, not so much at God or at you, but at the hopelessness of the situation, and at knowing there was nothing I could do, or say, or promise that would change your death and bring you back. There were times when I felt deeply and indescribably blue, and there were times when I felt like a two-year-old. When all I wanted was to sit on the floor kicking and screaming, "I want Don, I want Don," over and over again until God listened and allowed you to come back. I didn't care, of course, that it wouldn't work. Nothing worked. Not prayer. Not tears. Not even all my promises to be good.

I miss you. I really miss you even though it's been years since we've been together, but that was okay because I knew I could call you and you would be there for me. It breaks my heart that you are gone, not because I feel abandoned. I don't. I got over feeling that way. Maybe that's because you never abandoned me, or because of my therapy, or maybe it's because of the memoir I wrote. I just don't feel like that lost little girl anymore.

Even though we weren't together before you died, I wanted to see you again. I always wanted to see you again. But then you died, and when you died, death became a mountain between us.

After your death I missed you so much. I missed putting my head on your chest and listening to the sound of your heartbeat. I missed waking up in the middle of the night to listen to the sound of your breathing. I missed the sight of you. The physicality of you. I just missed you.

After you died there were so many things that reminded me too much of you. There were so many memories that came back to me. The day after I heard about your death I got into my car and started driving, revisiting all the places we had been to together. My first stop was to pass the house where I used to live and where you picked me up for our first date. I drove down the street, made a right and, after passing the synagogue, I arrived at the country inn where we went for dinner that night.

Thinking back, I remembered how nervous I was while waiting for you to arrive. I was sure I was going to say or do something so stupid I'd never see you again. When I woke up that morning (and I just found this in my journal), I woke up because my clock radio went off and I found myself listening to the sound of Elvis singing "The Wonder of You."

After dinner that night you took me home where we sat on the sofa talking quietly until I excused myself. When I returned, you were examining a book I had left on the coffee table. I told you about the literature/discussion class I was taking and about how beautifully that book was written. I didn't know it then, but you had a love for words stronger and more arduous than my own.

After passing the Inn that day after you died, I continued driving, moving through the industrial park and finally over the little bridge that led to your house. When I got there I saw that the blinds, which were always halfway up, were down now. *When he returns he won't be able to see outside,* I thought, and then I cried.

Once the dreams began, they continued. Not every night, but often. Sometimes I would wake up in the morning not remembering my dreams, but knowing we had been together all night long in some other place, in some other galaxy where we could play together, swinging from one star to another, or sitting together with our feet dangling over the edge of a moon.

Later, as time passed, I began to notice how your absence from my life was being replaced with moments during which I felt your presence, and as though the hours of my life were starting to come together and were expanding until I felt as though I was learning to transcend time, and as though all the days of my life had begun to flow gently, one into another, the way they did when we met – when day and night became but a single instant, a breathless moment in which I felt as though I was buoyed up and floating effortlessly through love's liquidity. I love you Don. I always have. I always will.

Today there were snowflakes floating past my windshield as I climbed into my bus for my afternoon run, reminding me of another long weekend when we were expecting a blizzard.

"We're getting two feet of snow this weekend," I said on the phone that Friday night, "I want to get snowed in with you."

"Well, come on over," you said and I did, stopping first to rent movies and buy groceries.

"What's your favorite movie?" I had asked the week before.

"*Unforgiven*," you replied. "What's yours?"

"*Moonstruck*."

"Is that the one that's so typically New York Italian?" you asked.

I laughed. "Yes. I love that movie."

On the way to your house for our lost weekend I stopped to pick up copies of each.

This year winter has been mild. It is almost the end of January, and we have yet to see a snowstorm or any more than an inch or two of snow. Today the temperatures were in the mid-forties, but this weekend temperatures are expected to plunge to below freezing. Next week will bring yet another anniversary of your death, but instead of mourning that now, I have decided I want to celebrate us by staying indoors and watching our favorite movies.

Thinking back, I can remember getting to your house that night and walking into the TV room where you were sitting in your rocking chair beside the window. I leaned down to kiss you as you grabbed my hand and held on to it. Later, I popped the first movie into the VCR.

We both fell silent at hearing the voice – that incredible voice - of Dean Martin singing "That's Amore" and at the sight of the Twin Towers standing in the moonlight.

The first time I watched *Moonstruck*, back in 1989, it reminded me of my early days growing up in Philadelphia. This weekend the movie kept reminding me of you.

"I can't sleep anymore. It's too much like death." Cosmo says early in the film, reminding me of your last couple of years, when you complained about waking up in the middle of the night and being unable to get back to sleep.

And then "I sleep too much," you said during one of our last conversations.

"It's okay," I said, "it's good for you."

Born half-Irish and half-German, you loved all things Italian, often laughing because you knew more Italian words and phrases than I did even though I was born with parents who talked to one another exclusively in Italian.

Knowing you had once been a plumber, I laughed when Rose said "There's my house," as she walked home from a restaurant with Perry.

"The whole house? It's a mansion."

"It's a house."

"What exactly does your husband do?"

"He's a plumber."

"Well, that explains it," Perry said.

And then I watched the climax of the movie. Again, two people, Loretta and Ronny, are walking home after their night at the opera. Ronny is pleading with Loretta to spend the night with him; Loretta is whining, worrying that if she does she will have bad luck. I don't know much about New York Italians, but here in Philadelphia we call a spade a spade, and bad luck is the evil eye. Or, as you might have said, "il malocchio."

I held my breath as Ronny launches into his soliloquy: "I love you. Not like they told you love is. And I didn't know this either, but love don't make things nice. It ruins everything. It breaks your heart. It makes things a mess. We aren't here to make things perfect. The snowflakes are perfect. The stars are perfect. Not us. Not us. We are here to ruin ourselves and to break our hearts and to love all the wrong people - and to die. The storybooks are bullshit!"

He was right of course, although I didn't know it then. I thought that love was perfect, that our love was perfect. And it was, but not in the storybook way. Not so we could live happily ever after. Love is perfect because it haunts us, and teaches us, and pushes us away from every one of our imperfections, and drives us toward the perfections of our souls.

It's midnight and I am standing by the window again, looking out at the snowflakes as they drift by me and disappear. Dearest Don, I have loved you for so many reasons, but most of all I love you because you opened your heart to me and let me walk in. Once inside, I never wanted to leave. But now standing by this window, I know it's time for me to leave, time for me to put down my pen and to move on. Know that no matter where I go, I'll remember you. Today, tomorrow, and forever. You are, and always have been, a part of me. Know too, that I am not afraid. As I move along the spiral that is time, I will keep ascending until I reach eternity, knowing that when it comes, it will come the way Y2K came – not as a shock, but as a whisper.

Loving you,

Toni

Acknowledgements

I want to thank all of the people – friends, family, and strangers who helped me through grief. All of the people mentioned in this book are real with the single exception of Father Chris, who is a composite of all the others, including and especially: my life counselor Barbara Weber who, even though she retired two weeks before my grief began, agreed to meet with me weekly afterward; and Rabbi Simcha Raphael, a stranger I met only once and completely by accident, but who helped me more than he knew.

I want also to give a special thank you to my children – Eric, Cynthia and Jessica – who read my manuscript and made suggestions, and are always there to cheer me on.

The Fifty-six Elvis Songs Included - or Alluded to - in Dear Elvis

Always On My Mind

An American Trilogy

Are You Lonesome Tonight

Blue Christmas

Blue Suede Shoes

Bridge over Troubled Water

Can't Help Falling in Love

Danny Boy

Don't

Don't Ask Me Why

Early Morning Rain

Edge of Reality

Fame and Fortune

Help Me Make It through the Night

Hound Dog

I Believe

I Feel that I've Known You Forever

I Just Can't Help Believin'

I Love You Because

I Miss You

I Need Somebody to Lean On

If Every Day was Like Christmas

If I Can Dream

If I Loved You

I'll Be There

I'll Remember You

Indescribably Blue

It Feels So Right

It's Midnight

It's Now or Never

Love Me Tender

Loving You

Make the World Go Away

Memories

Padre

Paralyzed

Pieces of my Life

So Lonesome I Could Cry

Soldier Boy

Snowbird

Tell Me Why

Today, Tomorrow and Forever

That's All Right

The First Time Ever I Saw Your Face

The Impossible Dream

The Last Farewell

The Wonder of You

They Remind Me Too Much of You

Unchained Melody

You Gave Me a Mountain

(You're So Square) Baby I Don't Care

Walk a Mile in my Shoes

We Can Make the Morning

What a Night

What Now My Love

Words

Made in the USA
Middletown, DE
15 December 2024